AT HOME ON THE EARTH

At Home on the Earth

A new selection of the later writings of Richard Jefferies

Selected and introduced by Jeremy Hooker

With illustrations by Agnes Miller Parker

Green Books

First published in 2001
by Green Books Ltd
Foxhole, Dartington
Totnes, Devon TQ9 6EB

Distributed in the USA by
Chelsea Green Publishing Company
PO Box 428, White River Junction, VT05001
(800) 639-4099 www.chelseagreen.com

Cover design by Rick Lawrence

Text printed by Biddles Ltd, Guildford, Surrey
on Five Seasons 100% recycled paper

British Library Cataloguing in Publication Data
available on request

ISBN 1 903998 02 6

Contents

Introduction

In his biography of Richard Jefferies, the poet Edward Thomas identified Jefferies with his native Wiltshire, describing him as 'the genius, the human expression, of this country, emerging from it, not to be detached from it any more than the curves of some statues from their maternal stone'. This perception of Jefferies as an 'earth spirit' or 'spirit of place' is a remarkable piece of myth-making, which tells us as much about Thomas as it does about Jefferies. To understand its significance it needs to be both set against the bare facts of Jefferies' life and seen in the light of his writing.

Richard Jefferies was born on a smallholding of about forty acres at Coate, near Swindon, in 1848. Unlike his son, Richard's father, who had to do a large part of the work of the struggling smallholding, did not see it as 'a pleasant one', and in 1878, during a period of agricultural depression when many people living on the land were forced to move to cities or to emigrate, he gave it up and went to live in Bath, where he became a jobbing gardener.

Richard's childhood was scarcely a settled one. Between the ages of four and nine he was virtually a foster-child, living with his aunt and uncle in Sydenham, and spending only a month at Coate each summer. Not surprisingly perhaps, he acquired the reputation of being a dreamy boy, who did not take an active part in farm work. He also started writing at quite an early age, and became a reporter on a local paper when he was seventeen. Thereafter Jefferies made a living, at times a precarious and never a prosperous one, as a journalist and author.

He made his reputation mainly as a writer about agriculture and life in the English countryside, providing, in part, vicarious experience for Londoners. After an unsuccessful start as a romantic novelist, he went on to produce several works of fiction, especially *Bevis* (1882) and *After London* (1885), and a spiritual autobiography, *The Story of My Heart* (1883), which became celebrated after his lifetime. Jefferies' health broke down towards the end of 1881, and he spent his remaining years, until his death in August 1887, in increasing pain. This was also the period in which he did some of his finest writing, combining natural observation with poignant recollection and mysticism.

The stance of most of Jefferies' writings is that of the individual explorer, 'discovering' the English countryside much as contemporary explorers were discovering previously 'unknown' areas of the world. As he explained in his essay 'Sport and Science', he fancied that England was 'an epitome of the natural world'; but he might as well have said Coate, for that was his microcosm. On the face of it, then, it may seem surprising that, after 1876, Jefferies never returned to Wiltshire to live. He resided with his family in a series of rented accommodations, in Surbiton from 1877 to 1882, in West Brighton from 1882 to 1884, in Eltham in 1884, in Rotherfield and then Crowborough in the following year, and at Goring from 1886 until his death. The pattern of his residences initially indicated his need to be near to London in order to pursue his career as an author and journalist, and latterly his search for health.

Jefferies was an idealist, who believed that "he who has got the sense of beauty in his eye can find it in things as they really are." "Idealize to the full," he advised, "but idealize the real." The fact of Jefferies' removal from Coate, and what he subsequently made of Coate as a writer, go some way towards explaining both the mythical figure he became for others and his own strong vein of idealism. What he would call 'the true English feeling for home life' informed his writing. Significantly he defined the feeling in an essay, 'After the County Franchise', which deals with the situation of people leaving their dwellings on the land as a result of agricultural depression. His own sense of home life owed everything to Coate.

In his bitter late essay, the posthumously published 'My Old Village', Jefferies said of himself as a boy, "I planted myself everywhere—in all the fields and under the trees", and it seems likely that the very insecurity of his early home life intensified his need to belong. Whether or not this was the case, Jefferies, as he describes in his fragment of autobiography (he treats the same experience fictionally in *Bevis*), formed an idea of Coate as "the centre of the world". Indeed, it was for him the centre of the cosmos. Here, the stars "were as much a part of my existence as the elms across the road, the house, the blue doors, the cattle shed, the meadow, and the brook. They were no more separated than the furniture of the parlour." On his home ground, Jefferies evidently experienced what Fritjof Capra calls "the mode of consciousness in which the individual feels connected to the cosmos as a whole".

This is not, I think, so different from the experience of other sensitive children, and perhaps especially those brought up in the country—it may even be seen as an expression of childhood *per se*, of the original undifferentiated sense of being part of the whole. In either context, it helps to explain Jefferies' attraction both for readers from similar backgrounds and for urban readers: indeed, for readers who bring to nature a strong need for a larger existence. Jefferies conveys to them the feeling that the natural world, both the man-made landscape and the world of earth, sea and stars, is the human home, and the home we share with all that lives. In Jefferies, however, this sense of original participation in the whole was qualified. As his thought developed he came to deny that there is a 'fit' between the human mind and nature, and to recognize "the old, old error: I love the earth; therefore the earth loves me—I am her child—I am Man, the favoured of all creatures. I am the centre, and all for me was made." Emotionally, Jefferies' range encompasses extremes of belonging and dispossession, and at both poles he sees nature humbly, whether as part of the whole or as a detached onlooker.

Jefferies was a great observer. He learned the art of observation as a boy from participatory (or predatory) activity—shooting and fishing—which he gave up for the greater pleasure of watching wild creatures. In effect he renounced power over nature, and submitted to the power of nature over his mind. The result was some of his best work—writing in which he works at looking, capturing something of the very life of nature, its quickness and abundance, its ceaseless activities and processes. Up to a point, the art he deploys could be seen as compensatory. In Jefferies' lifetime, with the growth of cities and the spread of modern communications, nature in England was contracting, and being marginalized. Jefferies, however, by concentrating on particular localities, including easily overlooked 'places' such as ditches and field corners, revealed the continuing and still largely unexplored life of 'wild England'.

The inclusiveness of Jefferies' feeling for home life—its embrace of everything from speck of dust to stars—makes it reasonable to view him as a great ecologist, in the original meaning of the word. In this respect, he still has a lot to teach us about the 'household' we are part of. He reminds us of the value of 'common' things; he teaches love and patience towards nature; he reminds us that everywhere is a 'centre'; he instructs us in practical approaches to nature, such as how to see through dark water. It would be a mistake, however, to overlook the fact that Jefferies was a man of his time, or to ignore the anthropocentric dimension of his thinking. As a youth he had read Plato and although he was later to say that he had "had to unlearn much of him", Platonic idealism was a constituent of his vision. To Jefferies, "Man's mind is the most important fact with which we are yet acquainted." The very fact of nature's lack of concern for Man intensified Jefferies' feeling for 'the ideal life of man'. This gives force to his passion for freedom and for enlargement, for opening the mind to awareness of its own potential, for gaining from nature's beauty an augmented sense of human possibility. On this subject, however, Jefferies could be a preacher, even a soapbox orator, and his mysticism could decline into Faustian or utopian rhetoric, and suggest a preoccupation with power that had more to do with the imperial spirit than with the power of nature. It should also be said, however, that his mysticism developed in conjunction with a generous and realistic politics, which argued for non-utilitarian values and for independence and mutual assistance.

Jefferies' pedagogy was constantly under pressure from his iconoclasm, and from the value he placed upon 'unlearning'. This was related to his ultimate refusal to impose his vision, or any human vision, on nature. Initially this was a matter of seeing that he could not see, because there is too much happening in nature, at any moment, for even the most acute observer to be able to see more than a fraction of what is taking place. From this recognition, Jefferies' iconoclasm extended to all ideas of natural order, which he replaced with his feeling "that there is no contracted order: there is divine chaos, and, in it, limitless hope and possibilities." With this belief he disposed equally of natural theology and contemporary scientific theories (though Jefferies greatly admired Darwin), and got rid of all ways of limiting nature's otherness to a human scheme or perception. Jefferies did, however, greatly value the iconoclastic work of contemporary science itself in "obliterating the superstitious past", and "coming to have a touch of that which is real". But his sense of the real was inseparable from magic, "the alchemy of nature".

Jefferies was a more varied writer than any selection could adequately show. Q. D. Leavis described him as "a many-sided and comprehensive genius". My selection aims to represent Jefferies mainly through his art as an essayist. The essay form is a permissive one, and Jefferies frequently takes advantage of its permissiveness, and rambles round and about his subject, much as a man walking or sitting still out-of-doors would see and remark on different things. It was also in his later essays, however, that Jefferies perfected his 'voice'. In some essays this is scarcely a metaphor, since Jefferies, when too ill to write, would dictate to his wife. The result was highly personal reflection, often poignant and occasionally sentimental, but usually transcending the self in the larger perspective. There is, I think, a qualitative difference between work that Jefferies did following the breakdown of his health in December 1881 and all but the very best of his earlier writing. But there is continuity, too, especially in his writing in pictures.

It has been suggested that Jefferies had an eidetic memory. Certainly he had an extraordinary sensitivity to visual impressions. Edward Thomas described this well:

> "The clearness of the physical is allied to the penetration of the spiritual vision. For both are nourished to their perfect flowering by the habit of concentration. To see a thing as he saw the sun-painted yellowhammer in Stewart's Mash is part of the office of the imagination. Imagination is no more than the making of graven images, whether of things on the earth or in the mind. To make them, clear concentrated sight and patient mind are the most necessary things after love, and these two are the children of love."

Jefferies' picture writing, or making of 'graven images', may be seen, at its most concentrated, as a form of prose poetry, and it places him among the poets and (to employ a term applied to Thoreau) great 'poet naturalists' of the nineteenth century, writers such as Dorothy Wordsworth, John Ruskin, Gerard Manley Hopkins and Thomas Hardy. Like Ruskin and Hardy, too, Jefferies developed his art of seeing into a moral vision. An excellent example of this is 'One of the New Voters', which describes "the realities of rural life behind the scenes". 'Primrose Gold in Our Village' is another example: we will not understand Jefferies unless we realize that the same man who wrote 'The Dawn' or *The Story of My Heart* also wrote this bitter and ironic exposure of cynical political manipulation.

Jefferies should also be recognized as a writer who, like Hopkins and Hardy, links his age to modernism. Jefferies' pictorial imagination (it is rarely mere word-painting) connects his most graphic writing to the imagism espoused by some novelists as well as poets around the time of the First World War. In fact, his influence on modern writing has been more significant than is generally recognized. It may be seen among naturalists who are also stylists, such as W. H. Hudson and Richard Mabey, on Henry Williamson, and, through Edward Thomas, on later poets.

Jefferies' writing had a profound influence upon Edward Thomas—not only through its imagery, but also through its rendering of a 'natural' speaking voice. The latter was as liberating for Thomas as was Robert Frost's example—Frost confirmed, in his poems, what Thomas had recognized in Jefferies' prose. Thomas, also, was Jefferies' most eloquent mythologist, as the quotation with which I began illustrates. We may see Thomas's perception of Jefferies as "the human expression" of his Wiltshire landscape as revealing Thomas's own frustrated need to belong. Looked at from a different angle, however, it contains an important truth. By seeing places with the sensitized eyes of a displaced man, and by observing nature humbly, with an art that recognized the inability of human thought to master or circumscribe 'divine chaos', Jefferies showed Thomas what it means to be at home on earth. It is what he has to show us too.

Jeremy Hooker

A Note on the Selection

'Autobiographical fragments' consist of Chapters 1 and 2 of *The Old House at Coate*, 1948. This book was edited by Samuel J. Looker, who gave the overall title to an unpublished Jefferies manuscript and divided it into chapters. Given the nature of the manuscript, and without disrespect to Looker, for whose promotion and editorial work on behalf of Jefferies all readers of Jefferies are greatly indebted, I decided to present the material in a form closer to the original. For 'Absence of Design in Nature', Chapter 7 of *The Old House at Coate*, I have retained Looker's title. Looker gave as the date of the manuscript 'probably *circa* 1884 or 1885'.

Subsequent to publication in journals, the following essays appeared in Jefferies' collections of papers, as follows: 'A Brook—A London Trout' and 'The Breeze on Beachy Head' in *Nature Near London*, 1883; 'A Roman Brook', 'The Pageant of Summer' and 'Meadow Thoughts' in *The Life of the Fields*, 1884; 'Wild Flowers', 'One of the New Voters', 'Out of Doors in February', 'Haunts of the Lapwing' and 'Red Roofs of London' in *The Open Air*, 1885; 'Hours of Spring', 'Nature and Books', 'Walks in the Wheat-Fields' and 'My Old Village' in *Field and Hedgerow*, 1889; 'The Sun and the Brook' in *The Hills and the Vale*, 1909. According to Edward Thomas, "The date of 'The Dawn' is uncertain. It may have been 1883, . . . or it may have been as late as 1885." Thomas published it for the first time in *The Hills and the Vale*. 'Primrose Gold in Our Village', first published in the *Pall Mall Gazette* in June 1887, was collected in *Field and Farm*, 1957.

The extract from Jefferies' notebook 1878-9 is taken from Walter Besant, *The Eulogy of Richard Jefferies*, 1888. The extract from the later notebook is taken from a transcript made by Phyllis Treitel. As much as possible, I have retained Jefferies' system of notations, including asterisks to mark points of special importance, and 'SL' (Sun Life or Soul Life) to introduce notes or ideas which he intended to work up into a book that would go beyond his thinking in *The Story of My Heart*. Initially I intended to represent this notebook exactly as Jefferies wrote it, but the impossibility of transcribing every detail of it accurately ruled this out. On second thoughts, I decided that both Jefferies and his readers would be best served by selections, which showed the struggle of his mind with the questions that preoccupied him, while omitting mere repetitions and textual obscurities that do not significantly add to what Jefferies is saying. The refusal to stop thinking for himself in the face of adversity is one of the things I most admire about Jefferies, and this is what the late notebook shows him doing, in great pain, towards the very end of his life. I have retained Jefferies' occasionally inconsistent spelling and idiosyncratic punctuation—all very much part of his 'speaking' style—from his other published writings.

I owe a particular debt of gratitude to Phyllis Treitel for showing me her transcription of the notebook and discussing it with me. Although responsibility for the selection rests with me alone, I am indebted to Professor W. J. Keith for both his published work on Jefferies and his personal communications to me, to Kim Taplin for our conversations about Jefferies over the years, and to Mieke, for her interest and practical support.

Jeremy Hooker

Autobiographical Fragments

I

THE OLD HOUSE at Coate, a little hamlet in Wiltshire, was shut off from the road by a solid stone wall, the general entrance being through double doors. They were called the blue doors, as that was the colour of the paint, and were between six and seven feet high. A favourite greyhound, when these doors (being hung on an incline) had closed behind his master, used to clear them at a bound, his paws seeming but just to touch the top so lightly did he go over. As the cross-bars slowly decayed and became hollow in places, robins and wrens came to them several times in the day for the insects. The tiny brown wrens appear to have their regular rounds, visiting the same spot day after day and always singing on the same perches. One used to sing on the top of these doors, and then passing on, first to the eaves of the cow-shed, next to a heap of stones, where he slipped through the interstices, then to some logs piled against the wall, sang again when he reached the woodpile, perched on the topmost faggot.

The eave-swallows dropping from their nests under the thatch and gaining impetus from the downward slide seemed as if they must strike the broad doors, but suddenly rising with sleight-of-wing passed over upwards into the buoyant air.

Intangible at hand, the blue yonder above the fields and the trees, like an ethereal lake, sustains these feathered swimmers with such ease that a stroke sends them an arrow's flight.

The doors were so high that when near them nothing could be seen beyond but the clouds, so that the sky seemed to linger at once, and the swallows rising over to dart with it. They faced the north, and the north side kept its paint well, but the inner southern side, burnt by the summer sun, and receiving the driving southern rain, decayed twice as fast.

The wagtails usually came, too, over these doors, uttering their call as they jerked up and down: the whole circuit of the place was open to them, yet they generally entered here. They were among the most constant of the residents, the dependants of the house. As they say in classical times, the slaves and the slaves' children, generation after generation, were sheltered by the same portico; so, though free to go wherever their wings can carry them, many species of birds cling to the homestead. Their nests are near it, they roost close at hand; by day they go out into the fields and forage but return every two or three hours, and are sure to meet some of their mates at the old place.

Opposite the blue doors, across the road, was a stile, and a footpath leading to a cattleyard, called the Lower Pen. That field was used for grazing, and rarely mown, so that there were generally cows in it. The wagtails, fond of feeding about cattle, jerking their tails up and down close to their very noses, got into the habit of leaving the homestead over the doors in this direction. First visiting the cows, and perhaps riding a few minutes on one's back, they went next to the yard at the Lower Pen, and presently returned the way they had come. They thus established a route, and continued to follow it.

The legs of the wagtail are so slender that they scarce seem capable of sustaining even its light weight; each appears a mere black line; the plumage is shaded with delicate precision, and every tiny feather besides that side or tip that meets the eye is equally carefully marked underneath, and where it cannot be observed, so much 'work' is there, so much thorough honesty in nature's art. Everything out of sight is as tenderly touched as that open to the passing view.

The wagtails, like the ibis, were sacred; they were never shot or disturbed; wagtails, swallows, swifts, turtle-doves, yellowhammers, robins, wrens, green plovers, and even thrushes, if not semi-sacred were rarely fired at.

One of the large blue doors was often 'hapsed', i.e. hasped open to the wall, for convenience of entrance and exit; but, when it was closed, the private road within made a pleasant ambulatory. On one side, the high wall of the front garden and of the house itself: on the other, that of the cattle-sheds, formed a kind of hollow way, shut at the end by the doors; these walls and doors kept off the hard easterly winds of spring, while the sunshine at midday filled the place with light and warmth. Walking up and down here, taking care not to go too near the doors, for some little draught, of course, drew over them as a wind draws back over a wood, the position of the sun could be marked as he rose higher day by day towards that degree which fills the fields with flowers. In winter, his disk but just cleared the top of the great oak, the largest in the first hedgerow southwards. Now he was as far again above the horizon, and the swallows were here—with no thought of nest-building, yet they come every now and then to perch on the ledge of the chimney (but just able to face the keen east) and twitter to each other. Another place they used to perch on was the ridge of the cattle-shed running parallel to the house. It was thatched, and, in course of time decaying, the sticks which are driven through the straw stood out an inch or so in a row along the summit of the roof. These little projections suited them; half a dozen or more sometimes settled there, marshalled in single file.

There were some very long willow poles leaning against the faggot pile; the points standing up high and isolated were continually visited by the swallows; so was the top of a tall pear in the orchard and an egg-plum tree; also the narrow steep ridge of the slated stable. All round the house they had their resting places, where they met to converse, or stayed to sing. They did not alight on trees in the hedgerows or copses; only close at home.

Walking to and fro here (the roadway was dry and firm underfoot), when going towards the doors and facing the north, the sky looked hard; and the elms by the Lower Pen could be seen to swing before the wind. On turning, the sunshine—the light itself seems warm—met me with its delicious touch: it is like bathing in a more delicate element; the southern sky was refulgent and could scarcely be gazed at; the grass of the meadow (on which the roadway opened after passing the buildings) was green, and the hedge on its right side budding into leaf.

The growth of the year from spring into summer is beautiful to watch. But when the north winds came and the lower sky and the trees appeared dark - everything darkens when the north wind blows, and the nights are black— this covered way was no longer tenable. It rushed straight through, making no account of the high doors; it came over and under and through them, and cleared every dead leaf and fibre and particle of dust, sweeping the place clean. The refrain of the wind sound changing—each page—with the seasons.

Then, turning to the left, I found some shelter behind the cart-house, and stable wall: not so good a strolling place, but better than none. If the breeze shifted south or west, quarters often cold in winter and spring, when the air blows full of moisture, there still remained the 'paving', as it was called: a broad footpath flagged by the house on the north side.

The swallows flew underneath, low down over the surface of the road. High as the great blue doors were, this leafy loophole flanked them. Years ago, it seemed an event when the second door was opened, not without labour, for the passage of the waggon. It had to be heaved off the central block, swung back, and propped there with the iron bar attached to it. The waggon came rolling in with a load of hay; wisps caught against the ivy; against the eaves even; the heavy weight made a deep sound, between the walls; the load, as it passed, shut out the light momentarily from the windows that fronted to the hollow way, and the top rose nearly level on to the roof there above the swallows' nests under the thatch.

II

THE sun rose in summer almost by the elms at the Lower Pen—across the road—so much to the north of east, and sank in the evening down the road which ran east and west, so that then the blue doors were shone on early in the morning for half an hour on their northern side; and one part (the rest being shaded by the projecting wall) I think was just touched by the sunset rays.

Seeing the sun thus day by day traverse the sky about the house, passing the fixed points corresponding to the compass, and changing his position with the seasons—so that the house, the garden, and the trees about it made one large sidereal dial—made the solar apparent motion and the phenomena of the heavens very real and almost tangible.

In summer, no matter how early in the morning we went to the corner of the wall, under the lime and the fir, to look over, there was the sun already high above the elms. He had started from over the level plain: rising with boldest curve almost to the zenith, the shadow of the house then scarcely covered the 'paving', and the moss on the northern slope of the thatched roof was dry under his beams: white and pulsing with heat, he looked straight down upon us: then descending steeply, as if it were a hill, he paused over the elms on Smith Field, and finally sank to the north of them, leaving but a mere notch of the earth to go under before the morning.

It looked about ten miles only from the spot where the disk went down to where it rose; and all the night, from half past ten till one o'clock, there was a faint white light just above where he travelled beneath. At a little after one it was lost in the fast coming dawn. The circle of the sun was almost visible; there was but a short arc wanting to complete it; and thus we saw and understood that the sun never sets.

And the advance of the sun up from the south, wheeling further towards us day by day as the spring came on: and the retreat, wheeling further away as the autumn came, was plain from the time when the disk just cleared—as I have said—the great oak in the first hedgerow to the south, till it rose and sank north of the line of the roadway, and at midday looked down right over the house. Here was the centre of the world, the sun swung round us; we rode at night straight away into the space of the stars.

On a dry summer night, when there was no dew, I used to lie down on my back at full length (looking to the east), on the grass footpath by the orchard, and gaze up into the sky. This is the only way to get at it and feel the stars: while you stand upright, the eye, and through the eye, the mind, is biased by the usual aspect of things: the house there, the trees yonder; it is difficult to forget the mere appearance of rising and setting. Looking straight up like this, from the path to the stars, it was clear and evident that I was really riding among them; they were not above, nor all round, but I was in the midst of them. There was no underneath, no above: everything was on a level with me; the sense of measurement and distance disappeared.

As one walks in a wood, with trees all about, so then by day (when the light only hid them) I walked amongst the stars. I had not got then to leave this world to enter space: I was already there. The vision is indeed contracted, nor can we lift our feet further than the earth; yet we are really among these things to-day. The eye sees further at night than at noon. But though the bright light of noon intervenes like a mist or cloud, still the stars are there, space is there and we are in the midst of it. The touch of the sun's rays seemed to make me feel to the sun; the sight of the stars, to make me feel to them.

Gazing up from the footpath at the points of light overhead, and at the openings between where the mind looks into space itself, there was nothing between me and them, nor between me and the sun. They were as much a part of my existence as the elms across the road, the house, the blue doors, the cattle-shed, the meadow, and the brook. They were no more separated than the furniture of the parlour; no more isolated than the table, the old, old chair where I used to sit, as it stood by the southern window, watching for the first star over the mulberry tree. The old chair was the furniture of the room; the elms and the grass and the bank were the furniture of the earth; the stars and the sun and the deep sky, the limitless ether, were only the continuation. There is no break, no chasm, between here and there; nothing to step over in the darkness of an inscrutable to-morrow. The light comes to us—the physical light—in that alone there is a connexion; the ether, too, extends; as for the mind, it can and does go farther than this. It does not require an ascent; we are there already. I have never felt so much myself, an individual, as a part of this whole. In the summer night, lying thus upon the grass, the faint, yet distinct, pole star shone on my left above an ash tree growing in the hedgerow across the road. It was always there, and still: but the stars of the Great Bear moved, and some of them (all the stars of the Lesser Bear) never sank: they revolved about the pole and never went under the horizon. From the Lesser Bear, which is the nearest, to the Great Bear is one step—a wider ring; from thence to Capella or Arcturus, a yet wider; and so on to the zenith and the south.

Thus I realized that none of the stars (nor the sun) ever rose or sank: and that gave the feeling of being among them. The sward on which I was lying, the orchard behind, the house, the white wall of the garden (the horse steadily feeding in the meadow), the elms, the blue doors and roadway, the cattle-shed, and the stile, with myself, were in the same stream of space.

In winter, at the beginning of the year, Orion rose up the road and over it, his huge glittering frame athwart the highway: then the Pleiades, a startled flock of sheep timidly running together, were over the elms by the rickyard: Antares, in summer, was low to the south, by the same great oak the sun just cleared in December: Arcturus often hung, night after night, over the orchard: Donati's Comet came, first, a tiny speck with a faint spray of light behind it, over the elms opposite the orchard (they were a favourite perch of the starlings that built in the thatch of the house), its flaming brand afterwards started forth from the sunset every evening.

One night there was a comet (after Donati's, it only appeared a short time) whose immense but thin and misty tail spanned the sky like a thicker Milky Way with stars shining through it.

The new moon usually appeared first over the hollow oak by the brook in Smith Field. The trees and the constellations were grouped together: by the boughs the march of Orion westward, as the spring went on, till he overtook the sun, was visible every night. Every year, at the same time, the same star shone through the same tree. The position of many of them, by day, was as well known to me as if I could have seen them: it was only to describe an imaginary arc from the top of the ash. The highest elm is but a little plant on the surface of the earth: no more than groundsel—a mere weed; you can see over the groundsel and the highest tree equally well. And the stars were but just above the ash and the oak—never far off, and always there.

The line of the sunlight, the edge between the shadow and the white beam, on the side of the window frame in the parlour—the southern window—moved every day. If I drew a pencil-mark along that line to-day, at two o'clock, and to-morrow, at two o'clock, there was a slight change; in a week, the mark was left far behind. Thus far, then, thus far subtended by the distance to the sun, my blue doors, and roadway, and mulberry tree and orchard, and meadow, had moved among the stars. I was among them already.

In the morning, the shadows of the elms by the rickyard on the east side of the roadway extended almost across the meadow: at noon, in summer, even the widespreading oak in the first hedgerow to the south scarcely darkened the grass beneath it; from a distance, the shadow was imperceptible—it did not, apparently, extend beyond the verge of the boughs. In the evening, the ashes and elms and oaks in the western hedge returned their shadows back across again to the rickyard.

As the seasons changed, the shadows moved round the field, only avoiding the northern end by the house. The shadows, too, as of the carthouse across the roadway, of the walnut tree where the roadway opened on the meadow, the slant from the garden wall across the blue doors: these shadows, too, every day and all day long, declared the motion, and the motion the inseparable connexion between the heavens and the ground underfoot. It was impossible to get away from it for a moment. If, while thinking of other things, I chanced to see a sunbeam on the wall: if I see it now, it instantly recalls the same feeling. Put your hand on it—you touch the sun; and know that you are as much in the ether, in space, as the sun itself.

Sometimes, at the northern end of my walk to and fro the roadway, look-ing over the blue doors, I saw the pale north sky from which the north wind rushed down and shook them, rattling the latch. Sometimes, returning to the other end, I saw the woods on the low hill southwards, two miles away, become hidden by a mist like cloud; in three minutes the shower came dri-ving up.

Or, another time, pausing by the wall of the house—for anything high helps you to look up—there were flecks of curling cloud, at an immense ele-vation, scarce moving, and hardly obscuring the blue—no more than lace.

Occasionally the white moon appeared in the azure sky of noonday. Again there was a faint mist, northwards over the blue doors; southwards, over the wooded slope; westwards (seen through the apple trees), over the slope there; eastwards, too, just a glimpse between the butts of the elms of the downs in that direction. A soft, delicious, mist—the summer air made visible—a mist that ripens the corn and fixes the fruit. Lie down, then, in the shadow, on the grass, in drowsy luxury.

There were loopholes in the trees, and openings between the buildings, look-out places from which in a moment I knew the state of the atmos-phere—they answered to the compass, they were fixed points of the observa-tory. But the view through each of these windows of the trees went farther than the fields, or the woods on the hills. The wind that came from the west through the apple trees, with scudding clouds and stormy sunsets lighting up the place with rosy glow, I could seem to see its course from rocky Cornwall, from the mountainous billows of the Atlantic, and yet farther and farther than the clear broad rivers of the new world, the vast Pacific opened its expanse.

Towards the east, lifting on tiptoe to glance over the blue doors, the blast which drove up in the face as if it were splashed with water, I could see its course, over the darkened fields and brooks, from the grey north sea, from the narrow inlets and fir woods of Scandinavia, and still east and north to the unknown ice. Southwards, through the rain mist that shut out the woods upon the hills, I could see the Solent, the green channel, the wide fields of France, the blue inland sea, the sands of Africa.

Like a vast plain seen from a hill the surface of the earth stretched around: it was mapped out from this, the centre, so vivid was the sense of seeing the whole. Yet, with all its size, it was small: too small.

I have always hoped that some day our voyagers will find the earth larger than is thought. I hope there are new continents somewhere: interminable forests, and mountains that will take a century to climb. With all its width, it seems so small: and it becomes less, daily, as we traverse it so easily. But it must always have been small to the thought. Scandinavia was just beyond the stile and the Lower Pen; Africa, just beyond the wooded slope; America, yonder over the bank. So large, and yet so little; so many thousand miles, yet seen at a glance in an instant.

Lying upon the sward at midnight, and looking up, as I have said, I felt but a speck: the house, the fields, the surface of the earth, stretching around, was scarce more than a clod rushing through space. There never seemed to me any distinction between day and night: it is a mere succession of light and shadow; but existence is continuous and knows no break. Neither is there any difference between the days: or, indeed, the years, or the centuries; it is all alike (I mean, to me); and what is meant by dates I could never grasp.

But though the great earth is small, the merest atom of lichen on the garden wall bounding the roadway, grey, rough to the touch, and fixed to the stone, is as real, it exists, and *is*, as much as if it filled half the visible horizon. It is very curious to touch anything; it is as if the soul thereby ascertained the existence of matter. From these windows of the trees, then, the world could be seen as well as the fields.

From a Notebook
October 16th 1878 to May 21st 1879

OCT. 16, 1878. – Wasp and very large blue-fly struggling, wrestling on leaf. In a few seconds wasp got the mastery, brought his tail round, and stung twice or thrice; then bit off the fly's proboscis, then the legs, then bit behind the head, then snipped off the wings, then fell off leaf, but flew with burden to the next, rolled the fly round, and literally devoured its intestines. Dropped off the leaf in its eager haste, got on third leaf, and continued till nothing was left but a small part of the body—the head had been snipped off before. This was one of those large black flies—a little blue underneath—not like meat flies, but bigger and squarer, that go to the ivy. Ivy in bloom close by, where, doubtless, the robber found his prey and seized it.

Surrey Oct. 27. – Redwings numerous, and good many fieldfares. Ivy, brown reddish leaves, and pale-green ribs.

Oct. 29. – Saw hawk perched on telegraph line out of railway-carriage window. Train passed by within ten yards: hawk did not move. Street mist. London, not fog, but on clear day comes up about two-thirds the height of the houses.

The horse-chestnut buds at end of boughs; tree quite bare of leaves; all sticky, colour of deep varnish, strongly adhesive. These showed on this tree very fully.

Golden-crested wren, pair together (Nov. 3); 'cheep-cheep' as they slipped about maple bush, and along and up oak bough; motions like the tree-creeper up a bough; the crest triangular, point towards beak, spot of yellow on wing. Still day: the earth holds its breath.

Nov. 11. – Gold-crested wren and tom-tit on furze clinging to the very spikes, and apparently busy on the tiny green buds now showing thickly on the prickles.

The contemplation of the star, the sun, the tree, raises the soul into a trance of inner sight of nature.

Nov. 17. – Sycamore leaves—some few still on—spotted with intensely black spots an inch across. Willow buds showing.

Nov. 23. – Oaks most beautiful in sun—elms nearly leafless, also beech and willow—but oaks still in full leaf, some light-brown, still trace of green, some brown, some buff, and tawny almost, save in background, toned by shadow, a trace of red. The elms hid them in summer; now the oaks stand out the most prominent objects everywhere, and are seen to be three times as numerous as expected.

Nov. 25. – Thrushes singing again; a mild day after a week or two cold.

Dec. 23. – Red-wings came within a yard, Velt came within ten, wood-pigeon the same. Weasel hunting hedge under snow; underground in ivy as busy as possible; good time for them.

Jan. 6. – Very sharp frost, calm, some sun in morning, dull at noon.

Jan. 7. – Frost, wind, dull.

Jan. 8. – Frost light, strong N.E. wind.

Jan. 9. – Frost light, some little snow, wind N.E., light.

Jan. 10. – Very fine, sunny, N.E. wind, sharp frosty morning.

   Orange moss on old tiles on cattle-sheds and barns a beautiful colour; a picture.

Feb. 7. – Larks soaring and singing the first time; one to an immense height; rain in morning, afternoon mild but a strong wind from west; catkins on hazel, and buds on some hazel-bushes; missel-thrush singing in copse; spring seems to have burst on us all at once; chaffinches pairing, or trying to; fighting.

Feb. 8. – Numerous larks soaring; copse quite musical; now the dull clouds of six weeks have cleared away, we see the sun has got up quite high in the sky at noon.

Feb. 12. – Rooks, five, wading into flood in meadow, almost up to their breasts; lark soaring and singing at half-past five, evening; light declining; partridges have paired. No blue geranium in Surrey that I have seen.

Feb. 17. – Rooks busy at nests, jackdaws at steeple; sliding down with wings extended 4.50 to gardens below at great speed.

Feb. 20. – Ploughs at work again; have not seen them for three months almost.

Feb. 21. – Snow three or four inches; broom bent down; the green stalks that stand up bent right down; afterwards bright sunshine for some hours, and then clouded again.

Feb. 22. – Berries on wild ivy on birch-tree, round and fully-formed and plentiful; berries not formed on garden ivy.

Feb. 27. – Snow on ground since morning of 21st; four wild ducks going over to east; first seen here for two years; larks fighting and singing over snow; thawing; snow disappeared during day; tom-tit at birch-tree buds; pigeons still in large flocks.

March 7. – Splendid day; warm sun; scarcely any wind; wood-pigeons calling in copse here.

April 16. – Elms beginning to get green with leaf-buds; apple leaf-buds opening green.

May 12: – A real May-day at last; warm, west wind, sunshine; birds singing as if hearts would burst; four or five blackbirds all in hearing at once; butterfly, small white, tipped with yellowish red; song of thrush more varied even than nightingale; if rare, people would go miles to hear it, never the same in same bird, and every bird different; fearless, too; *operatic* singer.

More stitchwort; now common; it looks like ten petals, but is really five; the top of the petal divided, which gives the appearance; a delicate beautiful white; leaves in pairs, pointed.

Humble-bees *do* suck cowslips.

May 14. – Lark singing beautifully in the still dark and clouded sky at a quarter to three o'clock in the morning; about twenty minutes afterwards the first thrush; thought I heard distant cuckoo—not sure; and ten minutes after that the copse by garden perfectly ringing with the music. A beautiful May morning; thoroughly English morning: southerly wind; warm, light breeze, smart showers of warm rain, and intervals of brilliant sunshine; the leaves in copse beautiful delicate green, refreshed, cleaned, and a still more lovely green from the shower; behind them the blue sky, and above the bright sun; white detached clouds sailing past. That is the morning; afternoon more cloudy.

More swifts later in evening. The first was flying low down against wind; seemed to progress from tip to tip of wing, alternately throwing himself along, now one tip downwards, now the other, like hand-over-hand swimming. Furze-chat, first in furze opposite, perched on high branch of furze above the golden blossom thick on that branch; a way of shaking wings while perched; 'chat-chat' low; head and part of neck black, white ring or band below, brownish general colour. Nightingale singing on elm-branch—a large, thick branch, projecting over the green by roadside—perched some twenty-five feet high. Yellowhammer noticed a day or two ago perched on branch lengthwise, not across. Oaks: more oaks out. Ash: thought I saw one with the large black buds enlarged and lengthened, but not yet burst.

May 18. – The white-throat feeds on the brink of the ditch, perching on fallen sticks or small bushes; there is then no appearance of a crest; afterwards he flies up to the topmost twig of the bush, or on a sapling tree, and immediately he begins to sing, and the feathers on the top of his head are all ruffled up, as if brushed the wrong way.

May 20. – Coo of dove in copse first.

May 21. – The flies teased in the lane today—the first time.

A Roman Brook

THE BROOK has forgotten me, but I have not forgotten the brook. Many faces have been mirrored since in the flowing water, many feet have waded in the sandy shallow. I wonder if any one else can see it in a picture before the eyes as I can, bright, and vivid as trees suddenly shown at night by a great flash of lightning. All the leaves and branches and the birds at roost are visible during the flash. It is barely a second; it seems much longer. Memory, like the lightning, reveals the pictures in the mind. Every curve, and shore, and shallow is as familiar now as when I followed the winding stream so often. When the mowing-grass was at its height, you could not walk far beside the bank; it grew so thick and strong and full of umbelliferous plants as to weary the knees. The life as it were of the meadows seemed to crowd down towards the brook in summer, to reach out and stretch towards the life-giving water. There the buttercups were taller and closer together, nails of gold driven so thickly that the true surface was not visible. Countless rootlets drew up the richness of the earth like miners in the darkness, throwing their petals of yellow ore broadcast above them. With their fulness of leaves the hawthorn bushes grow larger— the trees extend farther—and thus overhung with leaf and branch, and closely set about by grass and plant, the brook disappeared only a little way off, and could not have been known from a mound and hedge. It was lost in the plain of meads—the flowers alone saw it sparkle.

Hidden in those bushes and tall grasses, high in the trees and low on the ground there were the nests of happy birds. In the hawthorns blackbirds and thrushes built, often overhanging the stream, and the fledglings fluttered out into the flowery grass. Down among the stalks of the umbelliferous plants, where the grasses were knotted together, the nettle-creeper concealed her treasure, having selected a hollow by the bank so that the scythe should pass over. Up in the pollard ashes and willows here and there wood-pigeons built. Doves cooed in the little wooded enclosures where the brook curved almost round upon itself. If there was a hollow in the oak a pair of starlings chose it, for there was no advantageous nook that was not seized on. Low beside the willow stoles the sedge-reedlings built; on the ledges of the ditches, full of flags, moorhens made their nests. After the swallows had coursed long miles over the meads to and fro, they rested on the tops of the ashes and twittered sweetly. Like the flowers and grass, the birds were drawn towards the brook. They built by it, they came to it to drink; in the evening a grasshopper-lark trilled in a hawthorn bush. By night crossing the footbridge a star sometimes shone in the water underfoot. At morn and even the peasant girls came down to dip; their path was worn through the mowing-grass, and there was a flat stone let into the bank as a step to stand on. Though they were poorly habited, without one line of form or tint of colour that could please the eye, there is something in dipping water that is Greek—Homeric—something that carries the mind home to primitive times. Always the little children came with them; they too loved the brook like the grass and birds. They wanted to see the fishes dart away and hide in the green flags: they flung daisies and buttercups into the stream to float and catch awhile at the flags, and float again and pass away, like the friends of our boyhood, out of sight. Where there was pasture roan cattle came to drink, and horses, restless horses, stood for hours by the edge under the shade of ash trees. With what joy the spaniel plunged in, straight from the bank out among the flags—you could mark his course by seeing their tips bend as he brushed them swimming. All life loved the brook.

Far down away from roads and hamlets there was a small orchard on the very bank of the stream, and just before the grass grew too high to walk through I looked in the enclosure to speak to its owner. He was busy with his spade at a strip of garden, and grumbled that the hares would not let it alone, with all that stretch of grass to feed on. Nor would the rooks; and the moorhens ran over it, and the water-rats burrowed; the wood-pigeons would have the peas, and there was no rest from them all. While he talked and talked, far from the object in hand, as aged people will, I thought how the apple tree in blossom before us cared little enough who saw its glory. The branches were in bloom everywhere, at the top as well as at the side; at the top where no one could see them but the swallows. They did not grow for human admiration: that was not their purpose; that is our affair only—we bring the thought to the tree. On a short branch low down the trunk there hung the weather-beaten and broken handle of an earthenware vessel; the old man said it was a jug, one of the old folks' jugs—he often dug them up. Some were cracked, some nearly perfect; lots of them had been thrown out to mend the lane. There were some chips among the heap of weeds yonder. These fragments were the remains of Anglo-Roman pottery. Coins had been found— half a gallon of them—the children had had most. He took one from his pocket, dug up that morning; they were of no value, they would not ring. The labourers tried to get some ale for them, but could not; no one would take the little brass things. That was all he knew of the Cæsars: the apples were in fine bloom now, weren't they?

Fifteen centuries before there had been a Roman station at the spot where the lane crossed the brook. There the centurions rested their troops after their weary march across the downs, for the lane, now bramble-grown and full of ruts, was then a Roman road. There were villas, and baths, and fortifications; these things you may read about in books. They are lost now in the hedges, under the flowering grass, in the ash copses, all forgotten in the lane, and along the footpath where the June roses will bloom after the apple blossom has dropped. But just where the ancient military way crosses the brook there grow the finest, the largest, the bluest, and most lovely forget-me-nots that ever lover gathered for his lady.

The old man, seeing my interest in the fragments of pottery, wished to show me something of a different kind lately discovered. He led me to a spot where the brook was deep, and had somewhat undermined the edge. A horse trying to drink there had pushed a quantity of earth into the stream, and exposed a human skeleton lying within a few inches of the water. Then I looked up the stream and remembered the buttercups and tall grasses, the flowers that crowded down to the edge; I remembered the nests, and the dove cooing; the girls that came down to dip, the children that cast their flowers to float away. The wind blew the loose apple bloom and it fell in showers of painted snow. Sweetly the greenfinches were calling in the trees: afar the voice of the cuckoo came over the oaks. By the side of the living water, the water that all things rejoiced in, near to its gentle sound, and the sparkle of sunshine on it, had lain this sorrowful thing.

The Pageant of Summer

GREEN RUSHES, long and thick, standing up above the edge of the ditch, told the hour of the year as distinctly as the shadow on the dial the hour of the day. Green and thick and sappy to the touch, they felt like summer, soft and elastic, as if full of life, mere rushes though they were. On the fingers they left a green scent; rushes have a separate scent of green, so, too, have ferns, very different to that of grass or leaves. Rising from brown sheaths, the tall stems enlarged a little in the middle, like classical columns, and heavy with their sap and freshness, leaned against the hawthorn sprays. From the earth they had drawn its moisture, and made the ditch dry; some of the sweetness of the air had entered into their fibres, and the rushes—the common rushes—were full of beautiful summer. The white pollen of early grasses growing on the edge was dusted from them each time the hawthorn boughs were shaken by a thrush. These lower sprays came down in among the grass, and leaves and grass-blades touched. Smooth round stems of angelica, big as a gun-barrel, hollow and strong, stood on the slope of the mound, their tiers of well-balanced branches rising like those of a tree. Such a sturdy growth pushed back the ranks of hedge parsley in full white flower, which blocked every avenue and winding bird's-path of the bank. But the 'gix', or wild parsnip, reached already high above both, and would rear its fluted stalk, joint on joint, till it could face a man. Trees they were to the lesser birds, not even bending if perched on; but though so stout, the birds did not place their nests on or against them. Something in the odour of these umbelliferous plants, perhaps, is not quite liked; if brushed or bruised they give out a bitter greenish scent. Under their cover, well shaded and hidden, birds build, but not against or on the stems, though they will affix their nests to much less certain supports. With the grasses that overhung the edge, with the rushes in the ditch itself, and these great plants on the mound, the whole hedge was wrapped and thickened. No cunning of glance could see through it; it would have needed a ladder to help any one look over.

It was between the may and the June roses. The may bloom had fallen, and among the hawthorn boughs were the little green bunches that would feed the redwings in autumn. High up the briars had climbed, straight and towering while there was a thorn or an ash sapling, or a yellow-green willow, to uphold them, and then curving over towards the meadow. The buds were on them, but not yet open; it was between the may and the rose.

As the wind, wandering over the sea, takes from each wave an invisible portion, and brings to those on shore the ethereal essence of ocean, so the air lingering among the woods and hedges—green waves and billows—became full of fine atoms of summer. Swept from notched hawthorn leaves, broad-topped oak-leaves, narrow ash sprays and oval willows; from vast elm cliffs and sharp-taloned brambles under; brushed from the waving grasses and stiffening corn, the dust of the sunshine was borne along and breathed. Steeped in flower and pollen to the music of bees and birds, the stream of the atmosphere became a living thing. It was life to breathe it, for the air itself was life. The strength of the earth went up through the leaves into the wind. Fed thus on the food of the Immortals, the heart opened to the width and depth of the summer—to the broad horizon afar, down to the minutest creature in the grass, up to the highest swallow. Winter shows us Matter in its dead form, like the Primary rocks, like granite and basalt—clear but cold and frozen crystal. Summer shows us Matter changing into life, sap rising from the earth through a million tubes, the alchemic power of light entering the solid oak; and see! it bursts forth in countless leaves. Living things leap in the grass, living things drift upon the air, living things are coming forth to breathe in every hawthorn bush. No longer does the immense weight of Matter—the dead, the crystallized—press ponderously on the thinking mind. The whole office of Matter is to feed life—to feed the green rushes, and the roses that are about to be; to feed the swallows above, and us that wander beneath them. So much greater is this green and common rush than all the Alps.

Fanning so swiftly, the wasp's wings are but just visible as he passes; did he pause, the light would be apparent through their texture. On the wings of the dragon-fly as he hovers an instant before he darts there is a prismatic gleam. These wing textures are even more delicate than the minute filaments on a swallow's quill, more delicate than the pollen of a flower. They are formed of matter indeed, but how exquisitely it is resolved into the means and organs of life! Though not often consciously recognized, perhaps this is the great pleasure of summer, to watch the earth, the dead particles, resolving themselves into the living case of life, to see the seed-leaf push aside the clod and become by degrees the perfumed flower. From the tiny mottled egg come the wings that by-and-by shall pass the immense sea. It is in this marvellous transformation of clods and cold matter into living things that the joy and the hope of summer reside. Every blade of grass, each leaf, each separate floret and petal, is an inscription speaking of hope. Consider the grasses and the oaks, the swallows, the sweet blue butterfly—they are one and all a sign and token showing before our eyes earth made into life. So that my hope becomes as broad as the horizon afar, reiterated by every leaf, sung on every bough, reflected in the gleam of every flower. There is so much for us yet to come, so much to be gathered, and enjoyed. Not for you or me, now, but for our race, who will ultimately use this magical secret for their happiness. Earth holds secrets enough to give them the life of the fabled Immortals. My heart is fixed firm and stable in the belief that ultimately the sunshine and the summer, the flowers and the azure sky, shall become, as it were, interwoven into man's existence. He shall take from all their beauty and enjoy their glory. Hence it is that a flower is to me so much more than stalk and petals. When I look in the glass I see that every line in my face means pessimism; but in spite of my face—that is my experience—I remain an optimist. Time with an unsteady hand has etched thin crooked lines, and, deepening the hollows, has cast the original expression into shadow. Pain and sorrow flow over us with little ceasing, as the sea-hoofs beat on the beach. Let us not look at ourselves but onwards, and take strength from the leaf and the signs of the field. He is indeed despicable who cannot look onwards to the ideal life of man. Not to do so is to deny our birthright of mind.

The long grass flowing towards the hedge has reared in a wave against it. Along the hedge it is higher and greener, and rustles into the very bushes. There is a mark only now where the footpath was; it passed close to the hedge, but its place is traceable only as a groove in the sorrel and seed-tops. Though it has quite filled the path, the grass there cannot send its tops so high; it has left a winding crease. By the hedge here stands a moss-grown willow, and its slender branches extend over the sward. Beyond it is an oak, just apart from the bushes; then the ground gently rises, and an ancient pollard ash, hollow and black inside, guards an open gateway like a low tower. The different tone of green shows that the hedge is there of nut-trees; but one great hawthorn spreads out in a semicircle, roofing the grass which is yet more verdant in the still pool (as it were) under it. Next a corner, more oaks, and a chestnut in bloom. Returning to this spot an old apple tree stands right out in the meadow like an island. There seemed just now the tiniest twinkle of movement by the rushes, but it was lost among the hedge parsley. Among the grey leaves of the willow there is another flit of motion; and visible now against the sky there is a little brown bird, not to be distinguished at the moment from the many other little brown birds that are known to be about. He got up into the willow from the hedge parsley somehow, without being seen to climb or fly. Suddenly he crosses to the tops of the hawthorn and immediately flings himself up into the air a yard or two, his wings and ruffled crest making a ragged outline; jerk, jerk, jerk, as if it were with the utmost difficulty he could keep even at that height. He scolds, and twitters, and chirps, and all at once sinks like a stone into the hedge and out of sight as a stone into a pond. It is a whitethroat; his nest is deep in the parsley and nettles. Presently he will go out to the island apple tree and back again in a minute or two; the pair of them are so fond of each other's affectionate company they cannot remain apart.

Watching the line of the hedge, about every two minutes, either near at hand or yonder a bird darts out just at the level of the grass, hovers a second with labouring wings, and returns as swiftly to the cover. Sometimes it is a flycatcher, sometimes a greenfinch, or chaffinch, now and then a robin, in one place a shrike, perhaps another is a redstart. They are fly-fishing all of them, seizing insects from the sorrel tips and grass, as the kingfisher takes a roach from the water. A blackbird slips up into the oak and a dove descends in the corner by the chestnut tree. But these are not visible together, only one at a time and with intervals. The larger part of the life of the hedge is out of sight. All the thrush-fledglings, the young blackbirds, and finches are hidden, most of them on the mound among the ivy, and parsley, and rough grasses, protected too by a roof of brambles. The nests that still have eggs are not, like the nests of the early days of April, easily found; they are deep down in the tangled herbage by the shore of the ditch, or far inside the thorny thickets which then looked mere bushes, and are now so broad. Landrails are running in the grass concealed as a man would be in a wood; they have nests and eggs on the ground for which you may search in vain till the mowers come.

Up in the corner a fragment of white fur and marks of scratching show where a doe has been preparing for a litter. Some well-trodden runs lead from mound to mound; they are sandy near the hedge where the particles have been carried out adhering to the rabbits' feet and fur. A crow rises lazily from the upper end of the field, and perches in the chestnut. His presence, too, was unsuspected. He is there by far too frequently. At this season the crows are always in the mowing-grass, searching about, stalking in winding tracks from furrow to furrow, picking up an egg here and a foolish fledgling that has wandered from the mound yonder. Very likely there may be a moorhen or two slipping about under cover of the long grass; thus hidden, they can leave the shelter of the flags and wander a distance from the brook. So that beneath the surface of the grass and under the screen of the leaves there are ten times more birds than are seen.

Besides the singing and calling, there is a peculiar sound which is only heard in summer. Waiting quietly to discover what birds are about, I become aware of a sound in the very air. It is not the midsummer hum which will soon be heard over the heated hay in the valley and over the cooler hills alike. It is not enough to be called a hum, and does but just tremble at the extreme edge of hearing. If the branches wave and rustle they overbear it; the buzz of a passing bee is so much louder it overcomes all of it that is in the whole field. I cannot define it, except by calling the hours of winter to mind—they are silent; you hear a branch crack or creak as it rubs another in the wood, you hear the hoar frost crunch on the grass beneath your feet, but the air is without sound in itself. The sound of summer is everywhere—in the passing breeze, in the hedge, in the broad-branching trees, in the grass as it swings; all the myriad particles that together make the summer are in motion. The sap moves in the trees, the pollen is pushed out from grass and flower, and yet again these acres and acres of leaves and square miles of grass-blades—for they would cover acres and square miles if reckoned edge to edge—are drawing their strength from the atmosphere. Exceedingly minute as these vibrations must be, their numbers perhaps may give them a volume almost reaching in the aggregate to the power of the ear. Besides the quivering leaf, the swinging grass, the fluttering bird's wing, and the thousand oval membranes which innumerable insects whirl about, a faint resonance seems to come from the very earth itself. The fervour of the sunbeams descending in a tidal flood rings on the strung harp of earth. It is this exquisite undertone, heard and yet unheard, which brings the mind into sweet accordance with the wonderful instrument of nature.

By the apple tree there is a low bank, where the grass is less tall and admits the heat direct to the ground; here there are blue flowers—bluer than the wings of my favourite butterflies—with white centres—the lovely bird's-eyes, or veronica. The violet and cowslip, bluebell and rose, are known to thousands; the veronica is overlooked. The ploughboys know it, and the wayside children, the mower and those who linger in fields, but few else. Brightly blue and surrounded by greenest grass, imbedded in and all the more blue for the shadow of the grass, these growing butterflies' wings draw to themselves the sun. From this island I look down into the depth of the grasses. Red sorrel spires—deep drinkers of reddest sun wine—stand the boldest, and in their numbers threaten the buttercups. To these in the distance they give the gipsy-gold tint— the reflection of fire on plates of the precious metal. It will show even on a ring by firelight; blood in the gold, they say. Gather the open marguerite daisies, and they seem large—so wide a disc, such fingers of rays; but in the grass their size is toned by so much green. Clover heads of honey lurk in the bunches and by the hidden footpath. Like clubs from Polynesia the tips of the grasses are varied in shape: some tend to a point—the foxtails—some are hard and cylindrical; others, avoiding the club shape, put forth the slenderest branches with fruit of seed at the ends, which tremble as the air goes by. Their stalks are ripening and becoming of the colour of hay while yet the long blades remain green.

Each kind is repeated a hundred times, the foxtails are succeeded by fox-tails, the narrow blades by narrow blades, but never become monotonous; sor-rel stands by sorrel, daisy flowers by daisy. This bed of veronica at the foot of the ancient apple has a whole handful of flowers, and yet they do not weary the eye. Oak follows oak and elm ranks with elm, but the woodlands are pleas-ant; however many times reduplicated, their beauty only increases. So, too, the summer days; the sun rises on the same grasses and green hedges, there is the same blue sky, but did we ever have enough of them? No, not in a hundred years! There seems always a depth, somewhere, unexplored, a thicket that has not been seen through, a corner full of ferns, a quaint old hollow tree, which may give us something. Bees go by me as I stand under the apple, but they pass on for the most part bound on a long journey, across to the clover fields or up to the thyme lands; only a few go down into the mowing-grass. The hive bees are the most impatient of insects; they cannot bear to entangle their wings beating against grasses or boughs. Not one will enter a hedge. They like an open and level surface, places cropped by sheep, the sward by the roadside, fields of clover, where the flower is not deep under grass.

II

It is the patient humble-bee that goes down into the forest of the mowing-grass. If entangled, the humble-bee climbs up a sorrel stem and takes wing, without any sign of annoyance. His broad back with tawny bar buoy-antly glides over the golden buttercups. He hums to himself as he goes, so happy is he. He knows no skep, no cunning work in glass receives his labour, no artificial saccharine aids him when the beams of the sun are cold, there is no step to his house that he may alight in comfort; the way is not made clear for him that he may start straight for the flowers, nor are any sown for him. He has no shelter if the storm descends suddenly; he has no dome of twisted straw well thatched and tiled to retreat to. The butcherbird, with a beak like a crooked iron nail, drives him to the ground, and leaves him pierced with a thorn; but no hail of shot revenges his tortures. The grass stiffens at nightfall (in autumn), and he must creep where he may, if possibly he may escape the frost. No one cares for the humble-bee. But down to the flowering nettle in the mossy-sided ditch, up into the tall elm, winding in and out and round the branched buttercups, along the banks of the brook, far inside the deepest wood, away he wanders and despises nothing. His nest is under the rough grasses and the mosses of the mound, a mere tunnel beneath the fibres and matted surface. The hawthorn overhangs it, the fern grows by, red mice rus-tle past.

It thunders, and the great oak trembles; the heavy rain drops through the treble roof of oak and hawthorn and fern. Under the arched branches the lightning plays along, swiftly to and fro, or seems to, like the swish of a whip, a yellowish-red against the green; a boom! a crackle as if a tree fell from the sky. The thick grasses are bowed, the white florets of the wild parsley are beaten down, the rain hurls itself, and suddenly a fierce blast tears the green oak leaves and whirls them out into the fields; but the humble-bee's home, under moss and matted fibres, remains uninjured. His house at the root of the king of trees, like a cave in the rock, is safe. The storm passes and the sun comes out, the air is the sweeter and the richer for the rain, like verses with a rhyme; there will be more honey in the flowers. Humble he is, but wild; always in the field, the wood; always by the banks and thickets; always wild and humming to his flowers. Therefore I like the humble-bee, being, at heart at least, for ever roaming among the woodlands and the hills and by the brooks. In such quick summer storms the lightning gives the impression of being far more dangerous than the zigzag paths traced on the autumn sky. The electric cloud seems almost level with the ground and the livid flame to rush to and fro beneath the boughs as the little bats do in the evening.

Caught by such a cloud, I have stayed under thick larches at the edge of plantations. They are no shelter, but conceal one perfectly. The wood-pigeons come home to their nest trees; in larches they seem to have permanent nests, almost like rooks. Kestrels, too, come home to the wood. Pheasants crow, but not from fear—from defiance; in fear they scream. The boom startles them, and they instantly defy the sky. The rabbits quietly feed on out in the field between the thistles and rushes that so often grow in woodside pastures, quietly hopping to their favourite places, utterly heedless how heavy the echoes may be in the hollows of the wooded hills. Till the rain comes they take no heed whatever, but then make for shelter. Blackbirds often make a good deal of noise; but the soft turtle-doves coo gently, let the lightning be as savage as it will. Nothing has the least fear. Man alone, more senseless than a pigeon, put a god in vapour; and to this day, though the printing press has set a foot on every threshold, numbers bow the knee when they hear the roar the timid dove does not heed. So trustful are the doves, the squirrels, the birds of the branches, and the creatures of the field. Under their tuition let us rid ourselves of mental terrors, and face death itself as calmly as they do the livid lightning; so trustful and so content with their fate, resting in themselves and unappalled. If but by reason and will I could reach the godlike calm and courage of what we so thoughtlessly call the timid turtle-dove, I should lead a nearly perfect life.

The bark of the ancient apple tree under which I have been standing is shrunken like iron which has been heated and let cool round the rim of a wheel. For a hundred years the horses have rubbed against it while feeding in the aftermath. The scales of the bark are gone or smoothed down and level, so that insects have no hiding-place. There are no crevices for them, the horse-hairs that were caught anywhere have been carried away by birds for their nests. The trunk is smooth and columnar, hard as iron. A hundred times the mowing-grass has grown up around it, the birds have built their nests, the butterflies fluttered by, and the acorns dropped from the oaks. It is a long, long time, counted by artificial hours or by the seasons, but it is longer still in another way. The greenfinch in the hawthorn yonder has been there since I came out, and all the time has been happily talking to his love. He has left the hawthorn indeed, but only for a minute or two, to fetch a few seeds, and comes back each time more full of song-talk than ever. He notes no slow movement of the oak's shadow on the grass; it is nothing to him and his lady dear that the sun, as seen from his nest, is crossing from one great bough of the oak to another. The dew even in the deepest and most tangled grass has long since been dried, and some of the flowers that close at noon will shortly fold their petals. The morning airs, which breathe so sweetly, come less and less frequently as the heat increases. Vanishing from the sky, the last fragments of cloud have left an untarnished azure. Many times the bees have returned to their hives, and thus the index of the day advances. It is nothing to the greenfinches; all their thoughts are in their song-talk. The sunny moment is to them all in all. So deeply are they rapt in it that they do not know whether it is a moment or a year. There is no clock for feeling, for joy, for love.

And with all their motions and stepping from bough to bough, they are not restless; they have so much time, you see. So, too, the whitethroat in the wild parsley; so, too, the thrush that just now peered out and partly fluttered his wings as he stood to look. A butterfly comes and stays on a leaf—a leaf much warmed by the sun—and shuts his wings. In a minute he opens them, shuts them again, half wheels round, and by-and-by—just when he chooses, and not before—floats away. The flowers open, and remain open for hours, to the sun. Hastelessness is the only word one can make up to describe it; there is much rest, but no haste. Each moment, as with the greenfinches, is so full of life that it seems so long and so sufficient in itself. Not only the days, but life itself lengthens in summer. I would spread abroad my arms and gather more of it to me, could I do so.

All the procession of living and growing things passes. The grass stands up taller and still taller, the sheaths open, and the stalk arises, the pollen clings till the breeze sweeps it. The bees rush past, and the resolute wasps; the humble-bees, whose weight swings them along. About the oaks and maples the brown chafers swarm, and the fern-owls at dusk, and the blackbirds and jays by day, cannot reduce their legions while they last. Yellow butterflies, and white, broad red admirals, and sweet blues; think of the kingdom of flowers which is theirs! Heavy moths burring at the edge of the copse; green, and red, and gold flies: gnats, like smoke, around the tree-tops; midges so thick over the brook, as if you could haul a netful; tiny leaping creatures in the grass; bronze beetles across the path; blue dragonflies pondering on cool leaves of water-plantain. Blue jays flitting, a magpie drooping across from elm to elm; young rooks that have escaped the hostile shot blundering up into the branches; missel thrushes leading their fledglings, already strong on the wing, from field to field. An egg

here on the sward dropped by a starling; a red ladybird creeping, tortoise-like, up a green fern frond. Finches undulating through the air, shooting themselves with closed wings, and linnets happy with their young.

Golden dandelion discs—gold and orange—of a hue more beautiful, I think, than the higher and more visible buttercup. A blackbird, gleaming, so black is he, splashing in the runlet of water across the gateway. A ruddy kingfisher swiftly drawing himself, as you might draw a stroke with a pencil, over the surface of the yellow buttercups, and away above the hedge. Hart's-tongue fern, thick with green, so green as to be thick with its colour, deep in the ditch under the shady hazel boughs. White meadow-sweet lifting its tiny florets, and black-flowered sedges. You must push through the reed grass to find the sword-flags; the stout willow-herbs will not be trampled down, but resist the foot like underwood. Pink lychnis flowers behind the withy stoles, and little black moorhens swim away, as you gather it, after their mother, who has dived under the water-grass, and broken the smooth surface of the duckweed. Yellow loosestrife is rising, thick comfrey stands at the very edge; the sandpipers run where the shore is free from bushes. Back by the underwood the prickly and repellent brambles will presently present us with fruit. For the squirrels the nuts are forming, green beechmast is there—green wedges under the spray; up in the oaks the small knots, like bark rolled up in a dot, will be acorns. Purple vetches along the mounds, yellow lotus where the grass is shorter, and orchis succeeds to orchis. As I write them, so these things come—not set in gradation, but like the broadcast flowers in the mowing-grass.

Now follows the gorse, and the pink rest-harrow, and the sweet lady's-bedstraw, set as it were in the midst of a little thorn-bush. The broad repetition of the yellow clover is not to be written; acre upon acre, and not one spot of green, as if all the green had been planed away, leaving only the flowers to which the bees come by the thousand from far and near. But one white campion stands in the midst of the lake of yellow. The field is scented as though a hundred hives of honey had been emptied on it. Along the mound by it the bluebells are seeding, the hedge has been cut and the ground is strewn with twigs. Among those seeding bluebells and dry twigs and mosses I think a titlark has his nest, as he stays all day there and in the oak over. The pale clear yellow of charlock, sharp and clear, promises the finches bushels of seed for their young. Under the scarlet of the poppies the larks run, and then for change of colour soar into the blue. Creamy honeysuckle on the hedge around the cornfield, buds of wild rose everywhere; but no sweet petal yet. Yonder, where the wheat can climb no higher up the slope, are the purple heath-bells, thyme and flitting stonechats.

The lone barn shut off by acres of barley is noisy with sparrows. It is their city, and there is a nest in every crevice, almost under every tile. Sometimes the partridges run between the ricks, and when the bats come out of the roof, leverets play in the waggon-track. At even a fern-owl beats by, passing close to the eaves whence the moths issue. On the narrow waggon-track which descends along a coombe and is worn in chalk, the heat pours down by day as if an invisible lens in the atmosphere focussed the sun's rays. Strong woody knapweed endures it; so does toadflax and pale blue scabious, and wild mignonette. The very sun of Spain burns and burns and ripens the wheat on the edge of the coombe, and will only let the spring moisten a yard or two around it, but there a few rushes have sprung, and in the water itself brooklime with blue flowers grows so thickly that nothing but a bird could find space to drink. So down again from this sun of Spain to woody coverts where the wild hops are blocking every avenue, and green-flowered bryony would fain climb to the trees; where grey-flecked ivy winds spirally about the red rugged bark of pines, where burdocks fight for the footpath, and teazle-heads look over the low hedges. Brake-fern rises five feet high; in some way woodpeckers are associated with brake, and there seem more of them where it flourishes. If you count the depth and strength of its roots in the loamy sand, add the thickness of its flattened stem, and the width of its branching fronds, you may say that it comes near to be a little tree. Beneath where the ponds are bushy mare's-tails grow, and on the moist banks jointed pewterwort; some of the broad bronze leaves of water-weeds seem to try and conquer the pond and cover it so firmly that a wagtail may run on them. A white butterfly follows along the waggon-road, the pheasants slip away as quietly as the butterfly flies, but a jay screeches loudly and flutters in high rage to see us. Under an ancient garden wall among matted bines of trumpet convolvulus, there is a hedge-sparrow's nest overhung with ivy on which even now the last black berries cling.

There are minute white flowers on the top of the wall, out of reach, and lichen grows against it dried by the sun till it looks ready to crumble. By the gateway grows a thick bunch of meadow geranium, soon to flower; over the gate is the dusty highway road, quiet but dusty, dotted with the innumerable foot-marks of a flock of sheep that has passed. The sound of their bleating still comes back, and the bees driven up by their feet have hardly had time to settle again on the white clover beginning to flower on the short roadside sward. All the hawthorn leaves and briar and bramble, the honeysuckle, too, is gritty with the dust that has been scattered upon it. But see—can it be? Stretch a hand high, quick, and reach it down; the first, the sweetest, the dearest rose of June. Not yet expected, for the time is between the may and the roses, least of all here in the hot and dusty highway; but it is found—the first rose of June.

Straight go the white petals to the heart; straight the mind's glance goes back to how many other pageants of summer in old times! When perchance the sunny days were even more sunny; when the stilly oaks were full of mystery, lurking like the Druid's mistletoe in the midst of their mighty branches. A glamour in the heart came back to it again from every flower; as the sunshine was reflected from them so the feeling in the heart returned tenfold. To the dreamy summer haze love gave a deep enchantment, the colours were fairer, the blue more lovely in the lucid sky. Each leaf finer, and the gross earth enamelled beneath the feet. A sweet breath on the air, a soft warm hand in the touch of the sunshine, a glance in the gleam of the rippled waters, a whisper in the dance of the shadows. The ethereal haze lifted the heavy oaks and they were buoyant on the mead, the rugged bark was chastened and no longer rough, each slender flower beneath them again refined. There was a presence everywhere though unseen, on the open hills, and not shut out under the dark pines. Dear were the June roses then because for another gathered. Yet even dearer now with so many years as it were upon the petals; all the days that have been before, all the heart-throbs, all our hopes lie in this opened bud. Let not the eyes grow dim, look not back but forward; the soul must uphold itself like the sun. Let us labour to make the heart grow larger as we become older, as the spreading oak gives more shelter. That we could but take to the soul some of the greatness and the beauty of the summer!

Still the pageant moves. The song-talk of the finches rises and sinks like the tinkle of a waterfall. The greenfinches have been by me all the while. A bullfinch pipes now and then further up the hedge where the brambles and thorns are thickest. Boldest of birds to look at, he is always in hiding. The shrill tone of a goldfinch came just now from the ash branches, but he has gone on. Every four or five minutes a chaffinch sings close by, and another fills the interval near the gateway. There are linnets somewhere, but I cannot from the old apple tree fix their exact place. Thrushes have sung and ceased; they will begin again in ten minutes. The blackbirds do not cease; the note uttered by a blackbird in the oak yonder before it can drop is taken up by a second near the top of the field, and ere it falls is caught by a third on the left-hand side. From one of the topmost boughs of an elm there fell the song of a willow warbler for awhile; one of the least of birds, he often seeks the highest branches of the highest tree.

A yellowhammer has just flown from a bare branch in the gateway, where he has been perched and singing a full hour. Presently he will commence again, and as the sun declines will sing him to the horizon, and then again sing till nearly dusk. The yellowhammer is almost the longest of all the singers; he sits and sits and has no inclination to move. In the spring he sings, in the summer he sings, and he continues when the last sheaves are being carried from the wheat-field. The redstart yonder has given forth a few notes, the whitethroat flings himself into the air at short intervals and chatters, the shrike calls sharp and determined, faint but shrill calls descend from the swifts in the air. These descend, but the twittering notes of the swallows do not reach so far—they are too high to-day. A cuckoo has called by the brook, and now fainter from a greater distance. That the titlarks are singing I know, but not within hearing from here; a dove, though, is audible, and a chiffchaff has twice passed. Afar beyond the oaks at the top of the field dark specks ascend from time to time, and after moving in wide circles for awhile descend again to the corn. These must be larks; but their notes are not powerful enough to reach me, though they would were it not for the song in the hedges, the hum of innumerable insects, and the ceaseless "crake, crake" of landrails. There are at least two landrails in the mowing-grass; one of them just now seemed coming straight towards the apple tree, and I expected in a minute to see the grass move, when the bird turned aside and entered the tufts and wild parsley by the hedge. Thence the call has come without a moment's pause, "crake, crake", till the thick hedge seems filled with it. Tits have visited the apple tree over my head, a wren has sung in the willow, or rather on a dead branch projecting lower down than the leafy boughs, and a robin across under the elms in the opposite hedge. Elms are a favourite tree of robins—not the upper branches, but those that grow down the trunk, and are the first to have leaves in spring.

The yellowhammer is the most persistent individually, but I think the blackbirds when listened to are the masters of the fields. Before one can finish another begins, like the summer ripples succeeding behind each other, so that the melodious sound merely changes its position. Now here, now in the corner, then across the field, again in the distant copse, where it seems about to sink, when it rises again almost at hand. Like a great human artist, the blackbird makes no effort, being fully conscious that his liquid tone cannot be matched. He utters a few delicious notes, and carelessly quits the green stage of the oak till it pleases him to sing again. Without the blackbird, in whose throat the sweetness of the green fields dwells, the days would be only partly summer. Without the violet all the bluebells and cowslips could not make a spring, and without the blackbird, even the nightingale would be but half welcome. It is not yet noon, these songs have been ceaseless since dawn; this evening, after the yellowhammer has sung the sun down, when the moon rises and the faint stars appear, still the cuckoo will call, and the grasshopper lark, the landrail's "crake, crake" will echo from the mound, a warbler or a blackcap will utter his notes, and even at the darkest of the summer night the swallows will hardly sleep in their nests. As the morning sky grows blue, an hour before the sun, up will rise the larks singing and audible now, the cuckoo will recommence, and the swallows will start again on their tireless journey. So that the songs of the summer birds are as ceaseless as the sound of the waterfall which plays day and night.

I cannot leave it; I must stay under the old tree in the midst of the long grass, the luxury of the leaves, and the song in the very air. I seem as if I could feel all the glowing life the sunshine gives and the south wind calls to being. The endless grass, the endless leaves, the immense strength of the oak expanding, the unalloyed joy of finch and blackbird; from all of them I receive a little. Each gives me something of the pure joy they gather for themselves. In the blackbird's melody one note is mine; in the dance of the leaf shadows the formed maze is for me, though the motion is theirs; the flowers with a thousand faces have collected the kisses of the morning. Feeling with them, I receive some, at least, of their fulness of life. Never could I have enough; never stay long enough—whether here or whether lying on the shorter sward under the sweeping and graceful birches, or on the thyme-scented hills. Hour after hour, and still not enough. Or walking the footpath was never long enough, or my strength sufficient to endure till the mind was weary. The exceeding beauty of the earth, in her splendour of life, yields a new thought with every petal. The hours when the mind is absorbed by beauty are the only hours when we really live, so that the longer we can stay among these things so much the more is snatched from inevitable Time. Let the shadow advance upon the dial—I can watch it with equanimity while it is there to be watched. It is only when the shadow is *not* there, when the clouds of winter cover it, that the dial is terrible. The invisible shadow goes on and steals from us. But now, while I can see the shadow of the tree and watch it slowly gliding along the surface of the grass, it is mine. These are the only hours that are not wasted—these hours that absorb the soul and fill it with beauty. This is real life, and all else is illusion, or mere endurance. Does this reverie of flowers and waterfall and song form an ideal, a human ideal, in the mind? It does; much the same ideal that Phidias sculptured of man and woman filled with a god-like sense of the violet fields of Greece, beautiful beyond thought, calm as my turtle-dove before the lurid lightning of the unknown. To be beautiful and to be calm, without mental fear, is the ideal of nature. If I cannot achieve it, at least I can think it.

The Breeze on Beachy Head

THE WAVES coming round the promontory before the west wind still give the idea of a flowing stream, as they did in Homer's days. Here beneath the cliff, standing where beach and sand meet, it is still; the wind passes six hundred feet overhead. But yonder, every larger wave rolling before the breeze breaks over the rocks; a white line of spray rushes along them, gleaming in the sunshine; for a moment the dark rock-wall disappears, till the spray sinks.

The sea seems higher than the spot where I stand, its surface on a higher level—raised like a green mound—as if it could burst in and occupy the space up to the foot of the cliff in a moment. It will not do so, I know; but there is an infinite possibility about the sea; it may do what it is not recorded to have done. It is not to be ordered, it may overleap the bounds human observation has fixed for it. It has a potency unfathomable. There is still something in it not quite grasped and understood—something still to be discovered—a mystery.

So the white spray rushes along the low broken wall of rocks, the sun gleams on the flying fragments of the wave, again it sinks, and the rhythmic motion holds the mind, as an invisible force holds back the tide. A faith of expectancy, a sense that something may drift up from the unknown, a large belief in the unseen resources of the endless space out yonder, soothes the mind with dreamy hope.

The little rules and little experiences, all the petty ways of narrow life, are shut off behind by the ponderous and impassable cliff; as if we had dwelt in the dim light of a cave, but coming out at last to look at the sun, a great stone had fallen and closed the entrance, so that there was no return to the shadow. The impassable precipice shuts off our former selves of yesterday, forcing us to look out over the sea only, or up to the deeper heaven.

These breadths draw out the soul; we feel that we have wider thoughts than we knew; the soul has been living, as it were, in a nutshell, all unaware of its own power, and now suddenly finds freedom in the sun and the sky. Straight, as if sawn down from turf to beach, the cliff shuts off the human world, for the sea knows no time and no era; you cannot tell what century it is from the face of the sea. A Roman trireme suddenly rounding the white edge-line of chalk, borne on wind and oar from the Isle of Wight towards the grey castle at Pevensey (already old in olden days), would not seem strange. What wonder could surprise us coming from the wonderful sea?

The little rills winding through the sand have made an islet of a detached rock by the beach; limpets cover it, adhering like rivet-heads. In the stillness here, under the roof of the wind so high above, the sound of the sand draining itself is audible. From the cliff blocks of chalk have fallen, leaving hollows as when a knot drops from a beam. They lie crushed together at the base, and on the point of this jagged ridge a wheatear perches.

There are ledges three hundred feet above, and from these now and then a jackdaw glides out and returns again to his place, where, when still and with folded wings, he is but a speck of black. A spire of chalk still higher stands out from the wall, but the rains have got behind it and will cut the crevice deeper and deeper into its foundation. Water, too, has carried the soil from under the turf at the summit over the verge, forming brown streaks.

Upon the beach lies a piece of timber, part of a wreck; the wood is torn and the fibres rent where it was battered against the dull edge of the rocks. The heat of the sun burns, thrown back by the dazzling chalk; the river of ocean flows ceaselessly, casting the spray over the stones; the unchanged sky is blue.

Let us go back and mount the steps at the Gap, and rest on the sward there. I feel that I want the presence of grass. The sky is a softer blue, and the sun genial now the eye and the mind alike are relieved—the one of the strain of too great solitude (not the solitude of the woods), the other of too brilliant and hard a contrast of colours. Touch but the grass, and the harmony returns; it is repose after exaltation.

A vessel comes round the promontory; it is not a trireme of old Rome, nor the 'fair and stately galley' Count Arnaldus hailed with its seamen singing the mystery of the sea. It is but a brig in ballast, high out of the water, black of hull and dingy of sail: still, it is a ship, and there is always an interest about a ship. She is so near, running along but just outside the reef, that the deck is visible. Up rises her stern as the billows come fast and roll under; then her bow lifts, and immediately she rolls, and, loosely swaying with the sea, drives along.

The slope of the billow now behind her is white with the bubbles of her passage, rising, too, from her rudder. Steering athwart with a widening angle from the land, she is laid to clear the distant point of Dungeness. Next, a steamer glides forth, unseen till she passed the cliff; and thus each vessel that comes from the westward has the charm of the unexpected. Eastward there is many a sail working slowly into the wind, and as they approach talking in the language of flags with the watch on the summit of the Head.

Once now and then the great *Orient* pauses on her outward route to Australia, slowing her engines: the immense length of her hull contains every adjunct of modern life; science, skill, and civilization are there. She starts, and is lost sight of round the cliff, gone straight away for the very ends of the world. The incident is forgotten, when one morning, as you turn over the newspaper, there is the *Orient* announced to start again. It is like a tale of enchantment; it seems but yesterday that the Head hid her from view; you have scarcely moved, attending to the daily routine of life, and scarce recognize that time has passed at all. In so few hours has the earth been encompassed.

The seagulls as they settle on the surface ride high out of the water, like the mediaeval caravels, with their sterns almost as tall as the masts. Their unconcerned flight, with crooked wings unbent, as if it were no matter to them whether they flew or floated, in its peculiar jerking motion somewhat reminds one of the lapwing—the heron has it, too, a little—as if aquatic or water-side birds had a common and distinct action of the wing.

Sometimes a porpoise comes along, but just beyond the reef; looking down on him from the verge of the cliff, his course can be watched. His dark body, wet and oily, appears on the surface for two seconds; and then, throwing up his tail like the fluke of an anchor, down he goes. Now look forward, along the waves, some fifty yards or so, and he will come up, the sunshine gleaming on the water as it runs off his back, to again dive, and reappear after a similar interval. Even when the eye can no longer distinguish the form, the spot where he rises is visible, from the slight change in the surface.

The hill receding in hollows leaves a narrow plain between the foot of the sward and the cliff; it is ploughed, and the teams come to the footpath which follows the edge; and thus those who plough the sea and those who plough the land look upon each other. The one sees the vessel change her tack, the other notes the plough turning at the end of the furrow. Bramble bushes project over the dangerous wall of chalk, and grasses fill up the interstices, a hedge suspended in air; but be careful not to reach too far for the blackberries.

The green sea is on the one hand, the yellow stubble on the other. The porpoise dives along beneath, the sheep graze above. Green seaweed lines the reef over which the white spray flies, blue lucerne dots the field. The pebbles of the beach seen from the height mingle in a faint blue tint, as if the distance ground them into coloured sand. Leaving the footpath now, and crossing the stubble to 'France', as the wide open hollow in the down is called by the shepherds, it is no easy matter in dry summer weather to climb the steep turf to the furze line above.

Dry grass is as slippery as if it were hair, and the sheep have fed it too close for a grip of the hand. Under the furze (still far from the summit) they have worn a path—a narrow ledge, cut by their cloven feet—through the sward. It is time to rest; and already, looking back, the sea has extended to an indefinite horizon. This climb of a few hundred feet opens a view of so many miles more. But the ships lose their individuality and human character; they are so far, so very far, away, they do not take hold of the sympathies; they seem like sketches—cunningly executed, but only sketches—on the immense canvas of the ocean. There is something unreal about them.

On a calm day, when the surface is smooth as if the brimming ocean had been straked—the rod passed across the top of the measure, thrusting off the irregularities of wave; when the distant green from long simmering under the sun becomes pale; when the sky, without cloud, but with some slight haze in it, likewise loses its hue, and the two so commingle in the pallor of heat that they cannot be separated—then the still ships appear suspended in space. They are as much held from above as upborne from beneath.

They are motionless, midway in space—whether it is sea or air is not to be known. They neither float nor fly, they are suspended. There is no force in the flat sail, the mast is lifeless, the hull without impetus. For hours they linger, changeless as the constellations, still, silent, motionless, phantom vessels on a void sea.

Another climb up from the sheep path, and it is not far then to the terrible edge of that tremendous cliff which rises straighter than a ship's side out of the sea, six hundred feet above the detached rock below, where the limpets cling like rivet-heads, and the sand rills run around it. But it is not possible to look down to it—the glance of necessity falls outwards, as a raindrop from the eaves is deflected by the wind, because it *is* the edge where the mould crumbles; the rootlets of the grass are exposed; the chalk is about to break away in flakes.

You cannot lean over as over a parapet, lest such a flake should detach itself—lest a mere trifle should begin to fall, awakening a dread and dormant inclination to slide and finally plunge like it. Stand back; the sea there goes out and out, to the left and to the right, and how far is it to the blue overhead? The eye must stay here a long period, and drink in these distances, before it can adjust the measure, and know exactly what it sees.

The vastness conceals itself, giving us no landmark or milestone. The fleck of cloud yonder, does it part it in two, or is it but a third of the way? The world is an immense cauldron, the ocean fills it, and we are merely on the rim—this narrow land is but a ribbon to the limitlessness yonder. The wind rushes out upon it with wild joy; springing from the edge of the earth, it leaps out over the ocean. Let us go back a few steps and recline on the warm, dry turf.

It is pleasant to look back upon the green slope and the hollows and narrow ridges, with sheep and stubble and some low hedges, and oxen, and that old, old sloth—the plough—creeping in his path. The sun is bright on the stubble and the corners of furze; there are bees humming yonder, no doubt, and flowers, and hares crouching—the dew dried from around them long since, and waiting for it to fall again; partridges, too, corn-ricks, and the roof of a farmhouse by them. Lit with sunlight are the fields, warm autumn garnering all that is dear to the heart of man, blue heaven above—how sweet the wind comes from these!— the sweeter for the knowledge of the profound abyss behind.

Here, reclining on the grass— the verge of the cliff rising a little, shuts out the actual sea—the glance goes forth into the hollow unsupported. It is sweeter towards the corn-ricks, and yet the mind will not be satisfied, but ever turns to the unknown. The edge and the abyss recall us; the boundless plain, for it appears solid as the waves are levelled by distance, demands the gaze. But with use it becomes easier, and the eye labours less. There is a promontory standing out from the main wall, whence you can see the side of the cliff, getting a flank view, as from a tower.

The jackdaws occasionally floating out from the ledge are as mere specks from above, as they were from below. The reef running out from the beach, though now covered by the tide, is visible as you look down on it through the water; the seaweed, which lay matted and half dry on the rocks, is now under the wave. Boats have come round, and are beached; how helplessly little they seem beneath the cliff by the sea!

On returning homewards towards Eastbourne stay awhile by the tumulus on the slope. There are others hidden among the furze; butterflies flutter over them, and the bees hum round by day; by night the nighthawk passes, coming up from the fields and even skirting the sheds and houses below. The rains beat on them, and the storm drives the dead leaves over their low green domes; the waves boom on the shore far down.

How many times has the morning star shone yonder in the East? All the mystery of the sun and of the stars centres around these lowly mounds.

But the glory of these glorious Downs is the breeze. The air in the valleys immediately beneath them is pure and pleasant; but the least climb, even a hundred feet, puts you on a plane with the atmosphere itself, uninterrupted by so much as the tree-tops. It is air without admixture. If it comes from the south, the waves refine it; if inland, the wheat and flowers and grass distil it. The great headland and the whole rib of the promontory is wind-swept and washed with air; the billows of the atmosphere roll over it.

The sun searches out every crevice amongst the grass, nor is there the smallest fragment of surface which is not sweetened by air and light.

Underneath, the chalk itself is pure; and the turf thus washed by wind and rain, sun-dried and dew-scented, is a couch prepared with thyme to rest on. Discover some excuse to be up there always, to search for stray mushrooms— they will be stray, for the crop is gathered extremely early in the morning— or to make a list of flowers and grasses; to do anything, and, if not, go always without any pretext. Lands of gold have been found, and lands of spices and precious merchandise; but this is the land of health.

There is the sea below to bathe in, the air of the sky up hither to breathe, the sun to infuse the invisible magnetism of his beams. These are the three potent medicines of nature, and they are medicines that by degrees strengthen not only the body but the unquiet mind. It is not necessary to always look out over the sea. By strolling along the slopes of the ridge a little way inland there is another scene where hills roll on after hills till the last and largest hides those that succeed behind it.

Vast cloud-shadows darken one, and lift their veil from another; like the sea, their tint varies with the hue of the sky over them. Deep narrow valleys— lanes in the hills—draw the footsteps downwards into their solitude, but there is always the delicious air, turn whither you will, and there is always the grass, the touch of which refreshes. Though not in sight, it is pleasant to know that the sea is close at hand, and that you have only to mount to the ridge to view it. At sunset the curves of the shore westward are filled with a luminous mist.

Or if it should be calm, and you should like to look at the massive head-land from the level of the sea, row out a mile from the beach. Eastwards a bank of red vapour shuts in the sea, the wavelets—no larger than those raised by the oar—on that side are purple as if wine had been spilt upon them, but westwards the ripples shimmer with palest gold.

The sun sinks behind the summit of the Downs, and slender streaks of purple are drawn along above them. A shadow comes forth from the cliff; a duskiness dwells on the water; something tempts the eye upwards, and near the zenith there is a star.

Out of Doors in February

THE CAWING of the rooks in February shows that the time is coming when their nests will be reoccupied. They resort to the trees, and perch above the old nests to indicate their rights; for in the rookery possession is the law, and not nine-tenths of it only. In the slow dull cold of winter even these noisy birds are quiet, and as the vast flocks pass over, night and morning, to and from the woods in which they roost, there is scarcely a sound. Through the mist their black wings advance in silence, the jackdaws with them are chilled into unwonted quiet, and unless you chance to look up, the crowd may go over unnoticed. But so soon as the waters begin to make a sound in February, running in the ditches and splashing over stones, the rooks commence the speeches and conversations which will continue till late into the following autumn.

The general idea is that they pair in February, but there are some reasons for thinking that the rooks, in fact, choose their mates at the end of the preceding summer. They are then in large flocks, and if only casually glanced at appear mixed together without any order or arrangement. They move on the ground and fly in the air so close, one beside the other, that at the first glance or so you cannot distinguish them apart. Yet if you should be lingering along the by-ways of the fields as the acorns fall, and the leaves come rustling down in the warm sunny autumn afternoons, and keep an observant eye upon the rooks in the trees, or on the fresh-turned furrows, they will be seen to act in couples. On the ground couples alight near each other, on the trees they perch near each other, and in the air fly side by side. Like soldiers each has his comrade. Wedged in the ranks every man looks like his fellow, and there seems no tie between them but a common discipline. Intimate acquaintance with barrack or camp life would show that every one had his friend. There is also the mess, or companionship of half a dozen, a dozen, or more, and something like this exists part of the year in the armies of the rooks. After the nest time is over they flock together, and each family of three or four flies in concert. Later on they apparently choose their own particular friends; that is, the young birds do so. All through the winter after, say, October, these pairs keep together, though lost in the general mass to the passing spectator. If you alarm them while they are feeding on the ground in winter, supposing you have not got a gun, they merely rise up to the nearest tree, and it may then be observed that they do this in pairs. One perches on a branch and a second comes to him. When February arrives, and they resort to the nests to look after or seize on the property there, they are in fact already paired, though the almanacs put down St Valentine's day as the date of courtship.

There is very often a warm interval in February, sometimes a few days earlier and sometimes later, but as a rule it happens that a week or so of mild sunny weather occurs about this time. Released from the grip of the frost, the streams trickle forth from the fields and pour into the ditches, so that while walking along the footpath there is a murmur all around coming from the rush of water. The murmur of the poets is indeed louder in February than in the more pleasant days of summer, for then the growth of aquatic grasses checks the flow and stills it, whilst in February, every stone, or flint, or lump of chalk divides the current and causes a vibration. With this murmur of water, and mild time, the rooks caw incessantly, and the birds at large essay to utter their welcome of the sun. The wet furrows reflect the rays so that the dark earth gleams, and in the slight mist that stays farther away the light pauses and fills the vapour with radiance. Through this luminous mist the larks race after each other twittering, and as they turn aside, swerving in their swift flight, their white breasts appear for a moment. As while standing by a pool the fishes come into sight, emerging as they swim round from the shadow of the deeper water, so the larks dart over the low hedge, and through the mist, and pass before you, and are gone again. All at once one checks his pursuit, forgets the immediate object, and rises, singing as he soars. The notes fall from the air over the dark wet earth, over the dank grass, and broken withered fern of the hedges, and listening to them it seems for a moment spring. There is sunshine in the song; the lark and the light are one. He gives us a few minutes of summer in February days. In May he rises before as yet the dawn is come, and the sunrise flows down to us under through his notes. On his breast, high above the earth, the first rays fall as the rim of the sun edges up at the eastward hill. The lark and the light are as one, and wherever he glides over the wet furrows the glint of the sun goes with him. Anon alighting he runs between the lines of the green corn. In hot summer, when the open hillside is burned with bright light, the larks are then singing and soaring. Stepping up the hill laboriously, suddenly a lark starts into the light and pours forth a rain of unwearied notes overhead. With bright light, and sunshine, and sunrise, and blue skies the bird is so associated in the mind, that even to see him in the frosty days of winter, at least assures us that summer will certainly return.

Ought not winter, in allegorical designs, the rather to be represented with such things that might suggest hope than such as convey a cold and grim despair? The withered leaf, the snowflake, the hedging bill that cuts and destroys, why these? Why not rather the dear larks for one? They fly in flocks, and amid the white expanse of snow (in the south) their pleasant twitter or call is heard as they sweep along seeking some grassy spot cleared by the wind. The lark, the bird of the light, is there in the bitter short days. Put the lark then for winter, a sign of hope, a certainty of summer. Put, too, the sheathed bud, for if you search the hedge you will find the buds there, on tree and bush, carefully wrapped around with the case which protects them as a cloak. Put, too, the sharp needles of the green corn; let the wind clear it of snow a little way, and show that under cold clod and colder snow the green thing pushes up, knowing that summer must come. Nothing despairs but man. Set the sharp curve of the white new moon in the sky: she is white in true frost, and yellow a little if it is devising change. Set the new moon as something that symbols an increase. Set the shepherd's crook in a corner as a token that the flocks are already enlarged in number. The shepherd is the symbolic man of the hardest winter time. His work is never more important than then. Those that only roam the fields when they are pleasant in May, see the lambs at play in the meadow, and naturally think of lambs and May flowers. But the lamb was born in the adversity of snow. Or you might set the morning star, for it burns and burns and glitters in the winter dawn, and throws forth beams like those of metal consumed in oxygen. There is nought that I know by comparison with which I might indicate the glory of the morning star, while yet the dark night hides in the hollows. The lamb is born in the fold. The morning star glitters in the sky. The bud is alive in its sheath; the green corn under the snow; the lark twitters as he passes. Now these to me are the allegory of winter.

These mild hours in February check the hold which winter has been gaining, and as it were, tear his claws out of the earth, their prey. If it has not been so bitter previously, when this Gulf stream or current of warmer air enters the expanse it may bring forth a butterfly and tenderly woo the first violet into flower. But this depends on its having been only moderately cold before, and also upon the stratum, whether it is backward clay, or forward gravel and sand. Spring dates are quite different according to the locality, and when violets may be found in one district, in another there is hardly a woodbine-leaf out. The border line may be traced, and is occasionally so narrow, one may cross over it almost at a step. It would sometimes seem as if even the nut-tree bushes bore larger and finer nuts on the warmer soil, and that they ripened quicker. Any curious in the first of things, whether it be a leaf, or flower, or a bird, should bear this in mind, and not be discouraged because he hears some one else has already discovered or heard something.

A little note taken now at this bare time of the kind of earth may lead to an understanding of the district. It is plain where the plough has turned it, where the rabbits have burrowed and thrown it out, where a tree has been felled by the gales, by the brook where the bank is worn away, or by the sediment at the shallow places. Before the grass and weeds, and corn and flowers have hidden it, the character of the soil is evident at these natural sections without the aid of a spade. Going slowly along the footpath—indeed you cannot go fast in moist February—it is a good time to select the places and map them out where herbs and flowers will most likely come first. All the autumn lies prone on the ground. Dead dark leaves, some washed to their woody frames, short grey stalks, some few decayed hulls of hedge fruit, and among these the mars or stocks of the plants that do not die away, but lie as it were on the surface waiting. Here the strong teazle will presently stand high; here the ground-ivy will dot the mound with bluish-purple. But it will be necessary to walk slowly to find the

ground-ivy flowers under the cover of the briers. These bushes will be a likely place for a blackbird's nest; this thick close hawthorn for a bullfinch; these bramble thickets with remnants of old nettle stalks will be frequented by the whitethroat after a while. The hedge is now but a lattice-work which will before long be hung with green. Now it can be seen through, and now is the time to arrange for future discovery. In May everything will be hidden, and unless the most promising places are selected beforehand, it will not be easy to search them out. The broad ditch will be arched over, the plants rising on the mound will meet the green boughs drooping, and all the vacancy will be filled. But having observed the spot in winter you can almost make certain of success in spring.

It is this previous knowledge which invests those who are always on the spot, those who work much in the fields or have the care of woods, with their apparent prescience. They lead the new comer to a hedge, or the corner of a copse, or a bend of the brook, announcing beforehand that they feel assured something will be found there; and so it is. This, too, is one reason why a fixed observer usually sees more than one who rambles a great deal and covers ten times the space. The fixed observer who hardly goes a mile from home is like the man who sits still by the edge of a crowd, and by-and-by his lost companion returns to him. To walk about in search of persons in a crowd is well known to be the worst way of recovering them. Sit still and they will often come by. In a far more certain manner this is the case with birds and animals. They all come back. During a twelvemonth probably every creature would pass over a given locality: every creature that is not confined to certain places. The whole army of the woods and hedges marches across a single farm in twelve months. A single tree—especially an old tree—is visited by four-fifths of the birds that ever perch in the course of that period. Every year, too, brings something fresh, and adds new visitors to the list. Even the wild sea-birds are found inland, and some that scarce seem able to fly at all are cast far ashore by the gales. It is difficult to believe that one would not see more by extending the journey, but, in fact, experience proves that the longer a single locality is studied the more is found in it. But you should know the places in winter as well as in tempting summer, when song and shade and colour attract everyone to the field. You should face the mire and slippery path. Nature yields nothing to the sybarite. The meadow glows with buttercups in spring, the hedges are green, the woods lovely; but these are not to be enjoyed in their full significance unless you have traversed the same places when bare, and have watched the slow fulfilment of the flowers.

The moist leaves that remain upon the mounds do not rustle, and the thrush moves among them unheard. The sunshine may bring out a rabbit, feeding along the slope of the mound, following the paths or runs. He picks his way, he does not like wet. Though out at night in the dewy grass of summer, in the rain-soaked grass of winter, and living all his life in the earth, often damp nearly to his burrows, no time, and no succession of generations can make him like wet. He endures it, but he picks his way round the dead fern and the decayed leaves. He sits in the bunches of long grass, but he does not like the drops of rain or dew on it to touch him. Water lays his fur close, and mats it, instead of running off and leaving him sleek. As he hops a little way at a time on the mound he chooses his route almost as we pick ours in the mud and pools of February. By the shore of the ditch there still stand a few dry, dead dock stems, with some dry reddish-brown seed adhering. Some dry brown nettle stalks remain; some grey and broken thistles; some teazles leaning on the bushes. The power of winter has reached its utmost now, and can go no farther. These bines which still hang in the bushes are those of the greater bindweed, and will be used in a month or so by many birds as conveniently curved to fit about their nests. The stem of wild clematis, grey and bowed, could scarcely look more dead. Fibres are peeling from it, they come off at the touch of the fingers. The few brown feathers that perhaps still adhere where the flowers once were are stained and discoloured by the beating of the rain. It is not dead: it will flourish again ere long. It is the sturdiest of creepers, facing the ferocious winds of the hills, the tremendous rains that blow up from the sea, and bitter frost, if only it can get its roots into soil that suits it. In some places it takes the place of the hedge proper and becomes itself the hedge. Many of the trunks of the elms are swathed in minute green vegetation which has flourished in the winter, as the clematis will in the summer. Of all, the brambles bear the wild works of winter best. Given only a little shelter, in the corner of the hedges or under trees and copses they retain green leaves till the buds burst again. The frosts tint them in autumn with crimson, but not all turn colour or fall. The brambles are the bowers of the birds; in these still leafy bowers they do the courting of the spring, and under the brambles the earliest arum, and cleaver, or avens, push up. Round about them the first white nettle flowers, not long now; latest too, in the autumn. The white nettle sometimes blooms so soon (always according to locality), and again so late, that there seems but a brief interval between, as if it flowered nearly all the year round. So the berries on the holly if let alone often stay till summer is in, and new berries begin to appear shortly afterwards. The ivy, too, bears its berries far into the summer. Perhaps if the country be taken at large there is never a time when there is not a flower of some kind out, in this or that warm southern nook. The sun never sets, nor do the flowers ever die. There is life always, even in the dry fir-cone that looks so brown and sapless.

The path crosses the uplands where the lapwings stand on the parallel ridges of the ploughed field like a drilled company; if they rise they wheel as one, and in the twilight move across the fields in bands, invisible as they sweep near the ground, but seen against the sky in rising over the trees and the hedges. There is a plantation of fir and ash on the slope, and a narrow waggonway enters it, and seems to lose itself in the wood. Always approach this spot quietly, for whatever is in the wood is sure at some time or other to come to the open space of the track. Wood-pigeons, pheasants, squirrels, magpies, hares, everything feathered or furred, down to the mole, is sure to seek the open way. Butterflies flutter through the copse by it in summer, just as you or I might use the passage between the trees. Towards the evening the partridges may run through to join their friends before roost-time on the ground. Or you may see a covey there now and then, creeping slowly with humped backs, and at a distance not unlike hedgehogs in their motions. The spot therefore should be approached with care; if it is only a thrush out it is a pleasure to see him at his ease and, as he deems, unobserved. If a bird or animal thinks itself noticed it seldom does much, some will cease singing immediately they are looked at. The day is perceptibly longer already. As the sun goes down, the western sky often takes a lovely green tint in this month, and

one stays to look at it, forgetting the dark and miry way homewards. I think the moments when we forget the mire of the world are the most precious. After a while the green corn rises higher out of the rude earth.

Pure colour almost always gives the idea of fire, or rather it is perhaps as if a light shone through as well as colour itself. The fresh green blade of corn is like this, so pellucid, so clear and pure in its green as to seem to shine with colour. It is not brilliant—not a surface gleam or an enamel,—it is stained through. Beside the moist clods the slender flags arise filled with the sweetness of the earth. Out of the darkness under—that darkness which knows no day save when the ploughshare opens its chinks—they have come to the light. To the light they have brought a colour which will attract the sunbeams from now till harvest. They fall more pleasantly on the corn, toned, as if they mingled with it. Seldom do we realize that the world is practically no thicker to us than the print of our footsteps on the path. Upon that surface we walk and act our comedy of life, and what is beneath is nothing to us. But it is out from that under-world, from the dead and the unknown, from the cold moist ground, that these green blades have sprung. Yonder a steam-plough pants up the hill, groaning with its own strength, yet all that strength and might of wheels, and piston, and chains, cannot drag from the earth one single blade like these. Force cannot make it; it must grow—an easy word to speak or write, in fact full of potency. It is this mystery of growth and life, of beauty, and sweetness, and colour, starting forth from the clods that gives the corn its power over me. Somehow I identify myself with it; I live again as I see it. Year by year it is the same, and when I see it I feel that I have once more entered on a new life. And I think the spring, with its green corn, its violets, and hawthorn-leaves, and increasing song, grows yearly dearer and more dear to this our ancient earth. So many centuries have flown! Now it is the manner with all natural things to gather as it were by smallest particles. The merest grain of sand drifts unseen into a crevice, and by-and-by another; after a while there is a heap; a century and it is a mound, and then everyone observes and comments on it. Time itself has gone on like this; the years have accumulated, first in drifts, then in heaps, and now a vast mound, to which the mountains are knolls, rises up and overshadows us. Time lies heavy on the world. The old, old earth is glad to turn from the cark and care of drifted centuries to the first sweet blades of green.

There is sunshine to-day after rain, and every lark is singing. Across the vale a broad cloud-shadow descends the hillside, is lost in the hollow, and presently, without warning, slips over the edge, coming swiftly along the green tips. The sunshine follows—the warmer for its momentary absence. Far, far down in a grassy coombe stands a solitary cornrick, conical roofed, casting a lonely shadow—marked because so solitary, and beyond it on the rising slope is a brown copse. The leafless branches take a brown tint in the sunlight; on the summit above there is furze; then more hill lines drawn against the sky. In the tops of the dark pines at the corner of the copse, could the glance sustain itself to see them, there are finches warming themselves in the sunbeams. The thick needles shelter them from the current of air, and the sky is bluer above the pines. Their hearts are full already of the happy days to come, when the moss yonder by the beech, and the lichen on the fir-trunk, and the loose fibres caught in the fork of an unbending bough, shall furnish forth a sufficient mansion for their young. Another broad cloud-shadow, and another warm embrace of sunlight. All the serried ranks of the green corn bow at the word of command as the wind rushes over them.

There is largeness and freedom here. Broad as the down and free as the wind, the thought can roam high over the narrow roofs in the vale. Nature has affixed no bounds to thought. All the palings, and walls, and crooked fences deep down yonder are artificial. The fetters and traditions, the routine, the dull roundabout which deadens the spirit like the cold moist earth, are the merest nothings. Here it is easy with the physical eye to look over the highest roof. The moment the eye of the mind is filled with the beauty of things natural an equal freedom and width of view come to it. Step aside from the trodden footpath of personal experience, throwing away the petty cynicism born of petty hopes disappointed. Step out upon the broad down beside the green corn, and let its freshness become part of life.

The wind passes, and it bends—let the wind, too, pass over the spirit. From the cloud-shadow it emerges to the sunshine—let the heart come out from the shadow of roofs to the open glow of the sky. High above, the songs of the larks fall as rain—receive it with open hands. Pure is the colour of the green flags, the slender-pointed blades—let the thought be pure as the light that shines through that colour. Broad are the downs and open the aspect—gather the breadth and largeness of view. Never can that view be wide enough and large enough, there will always be room to aim higher. As the air of the hills enriches the blood, so let the presence of these beautiful things enrich the inner sense. One memory of the green corn, fresh beneath the sun and wind, will lift up the heart from the clods.

A Brook—a London Trout

SOME LOW wooden rails guarding the approach to a bridge over a brook one day induced me to rest under an aspen, with my back against the tree. Some horse-chestnuts, beeches, and alders grew there, fringing the end of a long plantation of willow stoles which extended in the rear following the stream. In front, southwards, there were open meadows and cornfields, over which shadow and sunshine glided in succession as the sweet westerly wind carried the white clouds before it.

The brimming brook, as it wound towards me through the meads, seemed to tremble on the verge of overflowing, as the crown of wine in a glass rises yet does not spill. Level with the green grass, the water gleamed as though polished where it flowed smoothly, crossed with the dark shadows of willows which leaned over it. By the bridge, where the breeze rushed through the arches, a ripple flashed back the golden rays. The surface by the shore slipped towards a side hatch and passed over in a liquid curve, clear and unvarying, as if of solid crystal, till shattered on the stones, where the air caught up and played with the sound of the bubbles as they broke.

Beyond the green slope of corn, a thin, soft vapour hung on the distant woods, and hid the hills. The pale young leaves of the aspen rustled faintly, not yet with their full sound; the sprays of the horse-chestnut, drooping with the late frosts, could not yet keep out the sunshine with their broad green. A white spot on the footpath yonder was where the bloom had fallen from a blackthorn bush.

The note of the tree-pipit came from over the corn—there were some detached oaks away in the midst of the field, and the birds were doubtless flying continually up and down between the wheat and the branches. A willow-wren sang plaintively in the plantation behind, and once a cuckoo called at a distance. How beautiful is the sunshine! The very dust of the road at my feet seemed to glow with whiteness, to be lit up by it, and to become another thing. This spot henceforward was a place of pilgrimage.

Looking that morning over the parapet of the bridge, down stream, there was a dead branch at the mouth of the arch, it had caught and got fixed while it floated along. A quantity of aquatic weeds coming down the stream had drifted against the branch and remained entangled in it. Fresh weeds were still coming and adding to the mass, which had attracted a water-rat.

Perched on the branch the little brown creature bent forward over the surface, and with its two forepaws drew towards it the slender thread of a weed, exactly as with hands. Holding the thread in the paws, it nibbled it, eating the sweet and tender portion, feeding without fear though but a few feet away, and precisely beneath me.

In a minute the surface of the current was disturbed by larger ripples. There had been a ripple caused by the draught through the arch, but this was now increased. Directly afterwards a moorhen swam out, and began to search among the edge of the tangled weeds. So long as I was perfectly still the bird took no heed, but at a slight movement instantly scuttled back under the arch. The water-rat, less timorous, paused, looked round, and returned to feeding.

Crossing to the other side of the bridge, up stream, and looking over, the current had scooped away the sand of the bottom by the central pier, exposing the brickwork to some depth—the same undermining process that goes on by the piers of bridges over great rivers. Nearer the shore the sand had silted up, leaving it shallow, where water-parsnip and other weeds joined, as it were, the verge of the grass and the stream. The sunshine reflected from the ripples on this, the southern side, continually ran with a swift, trembling motion up the arch.

Penetrating the clear water, the light revealed the tiniest stone at the bottom: but there was no fish, no water-rat, or moorhen on this side. Neither on that nor many succeeding mornings could anything be seen there; the tail of the arch was evidently the favourite spot. Carefully looking over that side again, the moorhen who had been out rushed back; the water-rat was gone. Were there any fish? In the shadow the water was difficult to see through, and the brown scum of spring that lined the bottom rendered everything uncertain.

By gazing steadily at a stone my eyes presently became accustomed to the peculiar light, the pupils adjusted themselves to it, and the brown tints became more distinctly defined. Then sweeping by degrees from a stone to another, and from thence to a rotting stick embedded in the sand, I searched the bottom inch by inch. If you look, as it were at large—at everything at once—you see nothing. If you take some object as a fixed point, gaze all around it, and then move to another, nothing can escape.

Even the deepest, darkest water (not, of course, muddy) yields after a while to the eye. Half close the eyelids, and while gazing into it let your intelligence rather wait upon the corners of the eye than on the glance you cast straight forward. For some reason when thus gazing the edge of the eye becomes exceedingly sensitive, and you are conscious of slight motions or of a thickness—not a defined object, but a thickness which indicates an object—which is otherwise quite invisible.

The slow feeling sway of a fish's tail, the edges of which curl over and grasp the water, may in this manner be identified without being positively seen, and the dark outline of its body known to exist against the equally dark water or bank. Shift, too, your position according to the fall of the light, just as in looking at a painting. From one point of view the canvas shows little but the presence of paint and blurred colour, from another at the side the picture stands out.

Sometimes the water can be seen into best from above, sometimes by lying on the sward, now by standing back a little way, or crossing to the opposite shore. A spot where the sunshine sparkles with dazzling gleam is perhaps perfectly impenetrable till you get the other side of the ripple, when the same rays that just now baffled the glance light up the bottom as if thrown from a mirror for the purpose. I convinced myself that there was nothing here, nothing visible at present—not so much as a stickleback.

Yet the stream ran clear and sweet, and deep in places. It was too broad for leaping over. Down the current sedges grew thickly at a curve; up the stream the young flags were rising; it had an inhabited look, if such a term may be used, and moorhens and water-rats were about but no fish. A wide furrow came along the meadow and joined the stream from the side. Into this furrow, at flood time, the stream overflowed farther up, and irrigated the level sward.

At present it was dry, its course, traced by the yellowish and white hue of the grasses in it only recently under water, contrasting with the brilliant green of the sweet turf around. There was a marsh marigold in it, with stems a quarter of an inch thick; and in the grass on the verge, but just beyond where the flood reached, grew the lilac-tinted cuckoo flowers, or cardamine.

The side hatch supplied a pond, which was only divided from the brook by a strip of sward not more than twenty yards across. The surface of the pond was dotted with patches of scum that had risen from the bottom. Part at least of it was shallow, for a dead branch blown from an elm projected above the water, and to it came a sedge-reedling for a moment. The sedge-reedling is so fond of sedges, and reeds, and thick undergrowth, that though you hear it perpetually within a few yards it is not easy to see one. On this bare branch the bird was well displayed, and the streak by the eye was visible; but he stayed there for a second or two only, and then back again to the sedges and willows.

There were fish I felt sure as I left the spot and returned along the dusty road, but where were they?

On the sward by the wayside, among the nettles and under the bushes, and on the mound the dark green arum leaves grew everywhere, sometimes in bunches close together. These bunches varied—in one place the leaves were all spotted with black irregular blotches; in another the leaves were without such markings. When the root leaves of the arum first push up they are closely rolled together in a pointed spike.

This, rising among the dead and matted leaves of the autumn, occasionally passes through holes in them. As the spike grows it lifts the dead leaves with it, which hold it like a ring and prevent it from unfolding. The force of growth is not sufficiently strong to burst the bond asunder till the green leaves have attained considerable size.

A little earlier in the year the chattering of magpies would have been heard while looking for the signs of spring, but they were now occupied with their nests. There are several within a short distance, easily distinguished in winter, but somewhat hidden now by the young leaves. Just before they settled down to housekeeping there was a great chattering and fluttering and excitement, as they chased each other from elm to elm.

Four or five were then often in the same field, some in the trees, some on the ground, their white and black showing distinctly on the level brown earth recently harrowed or rolled. On such a surface birds are visible at a distance; but when the blades of the corn begin to reach any height such as alight are concealed. In many districts of the country that might be called wild and lonely, the magpie is almost extinct. Once now and then a pair may be observed, and those who know their haunts can, of course, find them, but to a visitor passing through, there seems none. But here, so near the metropolis, the magpies are common, and during an hour's walk their cry is almost sure to be heard. They have, however, their favourite locality, where they are much more frequently seen.

Coming to my seat under the aspen by the bridge week after week, the burdocks by the wayside gradually spread their leaves, and the procession of the flowers went on. The dandelion, the lesser celandine, the marsh marigold, the coltsfoot, all yellow, had already led the van, closely accompanied by the purple ground-ivy, the red dead-nettle, and the daisy; this last a late comer in the neighbourhood. The blackthorns, the horse-chestnut, and the hawthorn came, and the meadows were golden with the buttercups.

Once only had I noticed any indication of fish in the brook; it was on a warm Saturday afternoon, when there was a labourer a long way up the stream, stooping in a peculiar manner near the edge of the water with a stick in his hand. He was, I felt sure, trying to wire a spawning jack, but did not succeed. Many weeks had passed, and now there came (as the close time for coarse fish expired) a concourse of anglers to the almost stagnant pond fed by the side hatch.

Well-dressed lads with elegant and finished tackle rode up on their bicycles, with their rods slung at their backs. Hoisting the bicycles over the gate into the meadow, they left them leaning against the elms, fitted their rods and fished in the pond. Poorer boys, with long wands cut from the hedge and ruder lines, trudged up on foot, sat down on the sward and watched their corks by the hour together. Grown men of the artisan class, covered with the dust of many miles' tramping, came with their luncheons in a handkerchief, and set about their sport with a quiet earnestness which argued long if desultory practice.

In fine weather there were often a dozen youths and four or five men standing, sitting, or kneeling on the turf along the shore of the pond, all intent on their floats, and very nearly silent. People driving along the highway stopped their traps, and carts, and vans a minute or two to watch them: passengers on foot leaned over the gate, or sat down and waited expectantly.

Sometimes one of the more venturesome anglers would tuck up his trousers and walk into the shallow water, so as to be able to cast his bait under the opposite bank, where it was deep. Then an ancient and much battered punt was discovered aground in a field at some distance, and dragged to the pond. One end of the punt had quite rotted away, but by standing at the other, so as to depress it there and lift the open end above the surface, two, or even three, could make a shift to fish from it.

The silent and motionless eagerness with which these anglers dwelt upon their floats, grave as herons, could not have been exceeded. There they were day after day, always patient and always hopeful. Occasionally a small catch—a mere 'bait'—was handed round for inspection; and once a cunning fisherman, acquainted with all the secrets of his craft, succeeded in drawing forth three perch, perhaps a quarter of a pound each, and one slender eel. These made quite a show, and were greatly admired; but I never saw the same man there again. He was satisfied.

As I sat on the white rail under the aspen, and inhaled the scent of the beans flowering hard by, there was a question which suggested itself to me, and the answer to which I never could supply. The crowd about the pond all stood with their backs to the beautiful flowing brook. They had before them the muddy banks of the stagnant pool, on whose surface patches of scum floated.

Behind them was the delicious stream, clear, and limpid, bordered with sedge and willow and flags, and overhung with branches. The strip of sward between the two waters was certainly not more than twenty yards; there was no division hedge, or railing, and evidently no preservation, for the mouchers came and washed their water-cress which they had gathered in the ditches by the side hatch, and no one interfered with them.

There was no keeper or water bailiff, not even a notice-board. Policemen, on foot and mounted, passed several times daily, and, like everybody else, paused to see the sport, but said not a word. Clearly, there was nothing whatever to prevent any of those present from angling in the stream; yet they one and all, without exception, fished in the pond. This seemed to me a very remarkable fact.

After a while I noticed another circumstance; nobody ever even looked into the stream or under the arches of the bridge. No one spared a moment from his float amid the scum of the pond, just to stroll twenty paces and glance at the swift current. It appeared from this that the pond had a reputation for fish, and the brook had not. Everybody who had angled in the pond recommended his friends to go and do likewise. There were fish in the pond.

So every fresh comer went and angled there, and accepted the fact that there were fish. Thus the pond obtained a traditional reputation, which circulated from lip to lip round about. I need not enlarge on the analogy that exists in this respect between the pond and various other things.

By implication it was evidently as much understood and accepted on the other hand that there was nothing in the stream. Thus I reasoned it out, sitting under the aspen, and yet somehow the general opinion did not satisfy me. There must be something in so sweet a stream. The sedges by the shore, the flags in the shallow, slowly swaying from side to side with the current, the sedge-reedlings calling, the moorhens and water-rats, all gave an air of habitation.

One morning, looking very gently over the parapet of the bridge (down stream) into the shadowy depth beneath, just as my eyes began to see the bottom, something like a short thick dark stick drifted out from the arch, somewhat sideways. Instead of proceeding with the current, it had hardly cleared the arch when it took a position parallel to the flowing water and brought up. It was thickest at the end that faced the stream; at the other there was a slight motion as if caused by the current against a flexible membrane, as it sways a flag. Gazing down intently into the shadow the colour of the sides of the fish appeared at first not exactly uniform, and presently these indistinct differences resolved themselves into spots. It was a trout, perhaps a pound and a half in weight.

His position was at the side of the arch, out of the rush of the current, and almost behind the pier, but where he could see anything that came floating along under the culvert. Immediately above him but not over was the mass of weeds tangled in the dead branch. Thus in the shadow of the bridge and in the darkness under the weeds he might easily have escaped notice. He was, too, extremely wary. The slightest motion was enough to send him instantly under the arch; his cover was but a foot distant, and a trout shoots twelve inches in a fraction of time.

The summer advanced, the hay was carted, and the wheat ripened. Already here and there the reapers had cut portions of the more forward corn. As I sat from time to time under the aspen, within hearing of the murmuring water, the thought did rise occasionally that it was a pity to leave the trout there till some one blundered into the knowledge of his existence.

There were ways and means by which he could be withdrawn without any noise or publicity. But, then, what would be the pleasure of securing him, the fleeting pleasure of an hour, compared to the delight of seeing him almost day by day? I watched him for many weeks, taking great precautions that no one should observe how continually I looked over into the water there. Sometimes after a glance I stood with my back to the wall as if regarding an object on the other side. If any one was following me, or appeared likely to peer over the parapet, I carelessly struck the top of the wall with my stick in such a manner that it should project, an action sufficient to send the fish under the arch. Or I raised my hat as if heated, and swung it so that it should alarm him.

If the coast was clear when I had looked at him still I never left without sending him under the arch in order to increase his alertness. It was a relief to know that so many persons who went by wore tall hats, a safeguard against their seeing anything, for if they approached the shadow of the tall hat reached out beyond the shadow of the parapet, and was enough to alarm him before they could look over. So the summer passed, and, though never free from apprehensions, to my great pleasure without discovery.

*   *   *

The sword-flags are rusting at their edges, and their sharp points are turned. On the matted and entangled sedges lie the scattered leaves which every rush of the October wind hurries from the boughs. Some fall on the water and float slowly with the current, brown and yellow spots on the dark surface. The grey willows bend to the breeze; soon the osier beds will look reddish as the wands are stripped by the gusts. Alone the thick polled alders remain green, and in their shadow the brook is still darker. Through a poplar's thin branches the wind sounds as in the rigging of a ship; for the rest, it is silence.

The thrushes have not forgotten the frost of the morning, and will not sing at noon; the summer visitors have flown and the moorhens feed quietly.

The plantation by the brook is silent, for the sedges, though they have drooped and become entangled, are not dry and sapless yet to rustle loudly. They will rustle dry enough next spring, when the sedge-birds come. A long withey-bed borders the brook and is more resorted to by sedge-reedlings, or sedge-birds, as they are variously called, than any place I know, even in the remotest country.

Generally it has been difficult to see them, because the withey is in leaf when they come, and the leaves and sheaves of innumerable rods hide them, while the ground beneath is covered by a thick growth of sedges and flags, to which the birds descend. It happened once, however, that the withey stoles had been polled, and in the spring the boughs were short and small. At the same time, the easterly winds checked the sedges, so that they were hardly half their height, and the flags were thin, and not much taller, when the sedge-birds came, so that they for once found but little cover, and could be seen to advantage.

There could not have been less than fifteen in the plantation, two frequented some bushes beside a pond near by, some stayed in scattered willows farther down the stream. They sang so much they scarcely seemed to have time to feed. While approaching one that was singing by gently walking on the sward by the roadside, or where thick dust deadened the footsteps, suddenly another would commence in the low thorn hedge on a branch, so near that it could be touched with a walking-stick. Yet though so near the bird was not wholly visible—he was partly concealed behind a fork of the bough. This is a habit of the sedge-birds. Not in the least timid, they chatter at your elbow, and yet always partially hidden.

If in the withey, they choose a spot where the rods cross or bunch together. If in the sedges, though so close it seems as if you could reach forward and catch him, he is behind the stalks. To place some obstruction between themselves and any one passing is their custom; but that spring, as the foliage was so thin, it only needed a little dexterity in peering to get a view. The sedge-bird perches aside, on a sloping willow rod, and, slightly raising his head, chatters, turning his bill from side to side. He is a very tiny bird, and his little eye looks out from under a yellowish streak. His song at first sounds nothing but chatter.

After listening a while the ear finds a scale in it—an arrangement and composition—so that, though still a chatter, it is a tasteful one. At intervals he intersperses a chirp, exactly the same as that of the sparrow, a chirp with a tang in it. Strike a piece of metal, and besides the noise of the blow, there is a second note, or tang. The sparrow's chirp has such a note sometimes, and the sedge-bird brings it in—tang, tang, tang. This sound has given him his country name of brook-sparrow, and it rather spoils his song. Often the moment he has concluded he starts for another willow stole, and as he flies begins to chatter when halfway across, and finishes on a fresh branch.

But long before this another bird has commenced to sing in a bush adjacent; a third takes it up in the thorn hedge; a fourth in the bushes across the pond; and from farther down the stream comes a faint and distant chatter. Ceaselessly the competing gossip goes on the entire day and most of the night; indeed, sometimes all night through. On a warm spring morning, when the sunshine pours upon the willows, and even the white dust of the road is brighter, bringing out the shadows in clear definition, their lively notes and quick motions make a pleasant commentary on the low sound of the stream rolling round the curve.

A moorhen's call comes from the hatch. Broad yellow petals of marsh-marigold stand up high among the sedges rising from the greyish-green ground, which is covered with a film of sun-dried aquatic grass left dry by the retiring waters. Here and there are lilac-tinted cuckoo-flowers, drawn up on taller stalks than those that grow in the meadows. The black flowers of the sedges are powdered with yellow pollen; and dark green sword-flags are beginning to spread their fans. But just across the road, on the topmost twigs of birch poles, swallows twitter in the tenderest tones to their loves. From the oaks in the meadows on that side titlarks mount above the highest bough and then descend, sing, sing, singing, to the grass.

A jay calls in a circular copse in the midst of the meadow; solitary rooks go over to their nests in the elms on the hill; cuckoos call, now this way and now that, as they travel round. While leaning on the grey and lichen-hung rails by the brook, the current glides by, and it is the motion of the water and its low murmur which renders the place so idle; the sunbeams brood, the air is still but full of song. Let us, too, stay and watch the petals fall one by one from a wild apple and float down on the stream.

But now in autumn the haws are red on the thorn, the swallows are few as they were in the earliest spring; the sedge-birds have flown, and the redwings will soon be here. The sharp points of the sword-flags are turned, their edges rusty, the forget-me-nots are gone. October's winds are too searching for us to linger beside the brook, but still it is pleasant to pass by and remember the summer days. For the year is never gone by; in a moment we can recall the sunshine we enjoyed in May, the roses we gathered in June, the first wheatear we plucked as the green corn filled. Other events go by and are forgotten, and even the details of our own lives, so immensely important to us at the moment, in time fade from the memory till the date we fancied we should never forget has to be sought in a diary. But the year is always with us; the months are familiar always; they have never gone by.

So with the red haws around and the rustling leaves it is easy to recall the flowers. The withey plantation here is full of flowers in summer; yellow iris flowers in June when midsummer comes, for the iris loves a thunder-shower. The flowering flag spreads like a fan from the root, the edges overlap near the ground, and the leaves are broad as sword-blades; indeed the plant is one of the largest that grows wild. It is quite different from the common flag with three grooves—bayonet shape—which appears in every brook. The yellow iris is much more local, and in many country streams may be sought for in vain, so that so fine a display as may be seen here seemed almost a discovery to me.

They were finest in the year of rain, 1879, that terrible year which is fresh in the memory of all who have any interest in out-of-door matters. At mid-summer the plantation was aglow with iris bloom. The large yellow petals were everywhere high above the sedge; in one place a dozen, then two or three, then one by itself, then another bunch. The marsh was a foot deep in water, which could only be seen by parting the stalks of the sedges, for it was quite hidden under them. Sedges and flags grew so thick that everything was concealed except the yellow bloom above.

One bunch grew on a bank raised a few inches above the flood which the swollen brook had poured in, and there I walked among them; the leaves came nearly up to the shoulder, the golden flowers on the stalks stood equally high. It was a thicket of iris. Never before had they risen to such a height; it was like the vegetation of tropical swamps, so much was everything drawn up by the continual moisture. Who could have supposed that such a downpour as occurred that summer would have had the effect it had upon flowers? Most would have imagined that the excessive rain would have destroyed them; yet never was there such floral beauty as that year. Meadow-orchis, buttercups, the yellow iris, all the spring flowers came forth in extraordinary profusion. The hay was spoiled, the farmers ruined, but their fields were one broad expanse of flower.

As that spring was one of the wettest, so that of the year in present view was one of the driest, and hence the plantation between the lane and the brook was accessible, the sedges and flags short, and the sedge-birds visible. There is a beech in the plantation standing so near the verge of the stream that its boughs droop over. It has a number of twigs around the stem—as a rule the beech-bole is clear of boughs, but some which are of rather stunted growth are fringed with them. The leaves on the longer boughs above fall off and voyage down the brook, but those on the lesser twigs beneath, and only a little way from the ground, remain on, and rustle, dry and brown, all through the winter.

Under the shelter of these leaves, and close to the trunk, there grew a plant of flag—the tops of the flags almost reached to the leaves—and all the winter through, despite the frosts for which it was remarkable, despite the snow and the bitter winds which followed, this plant remained green and fresh. From this beech in the morning a shadow stretches to a bridge across the brook, and in that shadow my trout used to lie. The bank under the drooping boughs forms a tiny cliff a foot high, covered with moss, and here I once observed shrew mice diving and racing about. But only once, though I frequently passed the spot; it is curious that I did not see them afterwards.

Just below the shadow of the beech there is a sandy, oozy shore, where the footprints of moorhens are often traceable. Many of the trees of the plantation stand in water after heavy rain; their leaves drop into it in autumn, and, being away from the influence of the current, stay and soak, and lie several layers thick. Their edges overlap, red, brown, and pale yellow, with the clear water above and shadows athwart it, and dry white grass at the verge. A horse-chestnut drops its fruit in the dusty road; high above its leaves are tinted with scarlet.

It was at the tail of one of the arches of the bridge over the brook that my favourite trout used to lie. Sometimes the shadow of the beech came as far as his haunts, that was early in the morning, and for the rest of the day the bridge itself cast a shadow. The other parapet faces the south, and looking down from it the bottom of the brook is generally visible, because the light is so strong. At the bottom a green plant may be seen waving to and fro in summer as the current sways it. It is not a weed or flag, but a plant with pale green leaves, and looks as if it had come there by some chance; this is the water-parsnip.

By the shore on this, the sunny side of the bridge, a few forget-me-nots grow in their season, water crow's-foot flowers, flags lie along the surface and slowly swing from side to side like a boat at anchor. The breeze brings a ripple, and the sunlight sparkles on it; the light reflected dances up the piers of the bridge. Those that pass along the road are naturally drawn to this bright parapet where the brook winds brimming full through green meadows. You can see right to the bottom; you can see where the rush of the water has scooped out a deeper channel under the arches, but look as long as you like there are no fish.

The trout I watched so long, and with such pleasure, was always on the other side, at the tail of the arch, waiting for whatever might come through to him. There in perpetual shadow he lay in wait, a little at the side of the arch, scarcely ever varying his position except to dart a yard up under the bridge to seize anything he fancied, and drifting out again to bring up at his anchorage. If people looked over the parapet that side they did not see him; they could not see the bottom there for the shadow, or if the summer noonday cast a strong beam even then it seemed to cover the surface of the water with a film of light which could not be seen through. There are some aspects from which even a picture hung on the wall close at hand cannot be seen. So no one saw the trout; if any one more curious leant over the parapet he was gone in a moment under the arch.

Folk fished in the pond about the verge of which the sedge-birds chattered, and but a few yards distant; but they never looked under the arch on the northern and shadowy side, where the water flowed beside the beech. For three seasons this continued. For three summers I had the pleasure to see the trout day after day whenever I walked that way, and all that time, with fishermen close at hand, he escaped notice, though the place was not preserved. It is wonderful to think how difficult it is to see anything under one's very eyes, and thousands of people walked actually and physically right over the fish.

However, one morning in the third summer, I found a fisherman standing in the road and fishing over the parapet in the shadowy water. But he was fishing at the wrong arch, and only with paste for roach. While the man stood there fishing, along came two navvies; naturally enough they went quietly up to see what the fisherman was doing, and one instantly uttered an exclamation. He had seen the trout. The man who was fishing with paste had stood so still and patient that the trout, reassured, had come out, and the navvy— trust a navvy to see anything of the kind—caught sight of him.

The navvy knew how to see through water. He told the fisherman, and there was a stir of excitement, a changing of hooks and bait. I could not stay to see the result, but went on, fearing the worst. But he did not succeed; next day the wary trout was there still, and the next, and the next. Either this particular fisherman was not able to come again, or was discouraged; at any rate, he did not try again. The fish escaped, doubtless more wary than ever.

In the spring of the next year the trout was still there, and up to the summer I used to go and glance at him. This was the fourth season, and still he was there; I took friends to look at this wonderful fish, which defied all the loafers and poachers, and above all, surrounded himself not only with the shadow of the bridge, but threw a mental shadow over the minds of passers-by, so that they never thought of the possibility of such a thing as trout. But one morning something happened. The brook was dammed up on the sunny side of the bridge, and the water let off by a side-hatch, that some accursed main or pipe or other horror might be laid across the bed of the stream somewhere far down.

Above the bridge there was a brimming broad brook, below it the flags lay on the mud, the weeds drooped, and the channel was dry. It was dry up to

the beech tree. There, under the drooping boughs of the beech, was a small
pool of muddy water, perhaps two yards long, and very narrow—a stagnant
muddy pool, not more than three or four inches deep. In this I saw the trout.
In the shallow water, his back came up to the surface (for his fins must have
touched the mud sometimes)—once it came above the surface, and his spots
showed as plain as if you had held him in your hand. He was swimming
round to try and find out the reason of this sudden stinting of room.

Twice he heaved himself somewhat on his side over a dead branch that was
at the bottom, and exhibited all his beauty to the air and sunshine. Then he
went away into another part of the shallow and was hidden by the muddy
water. Now under the arch of the bridge, his favourite arch, close by there was
a deep pool, for, as already mentioned, the scour of the current scooped away
the sand and made a hole there. When the stream was shut off by the dam
above this hole remained partly full. Between this pool and the shallow under
the beech there was sufficient connection for the fish to move into it.

My only hope was that he would do so, and as some showers fell, tem-
porarily increasing the depth of the narrow canal between the two pools, there
seemed every reason to believe that he had got to that under the arch. If now
only that accursed pipe or main, or whatever repair it was, could be finished
quickly, even now the trout might escape! Every day my anxiety increased, for
the intelligence would soon get about that the brook was dammed up, and
any pools left in it would be sure to attract attention.

Sunday came, and directly the bells had done ringing four men attacked
the pool under the arch. They took off shoes and stockings and waded in, two
at each end of the arch. Stuck in the mud close by was an eel-spear. They
churned up the mud, wading in, and thickened and darkened it as they
groped under. No one could watch these barbarians longer.

Is it possible that he could have escaped? He was a wonderful fish, wary
and quick. Is it just possible that they may not even have known that a trout
was there at all; but have merely hoped for perch, or tench, or eels? The pool
was deep and the fish quick—they did not bale it, might he have escaped?
Might they even, if they did find him, have mercifully taken him and placed
him alive in some other water nearer their homes? Is it possible that he may
have almost miraculously made his way down the stream into other pools?

There was very heavy rain one night, which might have given him such a
chance. These 'mights', and 'ifs', and 'is it possible' even now keep alive some
little hope that some day I may yet see him again. But that was in the early
summer. It is now winter, and the beech has brown spots. Among the limes
the sedges are matted and entangled, the sword-flags rusty; the rooks are at
the acorns, and the plough is at work in the stubble. I have never seen him

since. I never failed to glance over the parapet into the shadowy water. Somehow it seemed to look colder, darker, less pleasant than it used to do. The spot was empty, and the shrill winds whistled through the poplars.

Haunts of the Lapwing

Winter

COMING LIKE a white wall the rain reaches me, and in an instant everything is gone from sight that is more than ten yards distant. The narrow upland road is beaten to a darker hue, and two runnels of water rush along at the sides, where, when the chalk-laden streamlets dry, blue splinters of flint will be exposed in the channels. For a moment the air seems driven away by the sudden pressure, and I catch my breath and stand still with one shoulder forward to receive the blow. Hiss, the land shudders under the cold onslaught; hiss, and on the blast goes, and the sound with it, for the very fury of the rain, after the first second, drowns its own noise. There is not a single creature visible, the low and stunted hedgerows, bare of leaf, could conceal nothing; the

rain passes straight through to the ground. Crooked and gnarled, the bushes are locked together as if in no other way could they hold themselves against the gales. Such little grass as there is on the mounds is thin and short, and could not hide a mouse. There is no finch, sparrow, thrush, blackbird. As the wave of rain passes over and leaves a hollow between the waters, that which has gone and that to come, the ploughed lands on either side are seen to be equally bare. In furrows full of water, a hare would not sit, nor partridge run; the larks, the patient larks which endure almost everything, even they have gone. Furrow on furrow with flints dotted on their slopes, and chalk lumps, that is all. The cold earth gives no sweet petal of flower, nor can any bud of thought or bloom of imagination start forth in the mind. But step by step, forcing a way through the rain and over the ridge, I find a small and stunted copse down in the next hollow. It is rather a wide hedge than a copse, and stands by the road in the corner of a field. The boughs are bare; still they break the storm, and it is a relief to wait a while there and rest. After a minute or so the eye gets accustomed to the branches and finds a line of sight through the narrow end of the copse. Within twenty yards—just outside the copse—there are a number of lapwings, dispersed about the furrows. One runs a few feet forward and picks something from the ground; another runs in the same manner to one side; a third rushes in still a third direction. Their crests, their green-tinted wings, and white breasts are not disarranged by the torrent. Something in the style of the birds recalls the wagtail, though they are so much larger. Beyond these are half a dozen more, and in a straggling line others extend out into the field. They have found some slight shelter here from the sweeping of the rain and wind, and are not obliged to face it as in the open. Minutely searching every clod they gather their food in imperceptible items from the surface.

Sodden leaves lie in the furrows along the side of the copse; broken and decaying burdocks still uphold their jagged stems, but will be soaked away by degrees; dank grasses droop outwards; the red seed of a dock is all that remains of the berries and fruit, the seeds and grain of autumn. Like the hedge, the copse is vacant. Nothing moves within, watch as carefully as I may. The boughs are blackened by wet and would touch cold. From the grasses to the branches there is nothing any one would like to handle, and I stand apart even from the bush that keeps away the rain. The green plovers are the only things of life that save the earth from utter loneliness. Heavily as the rain may fall, cold as the saturated wind may blow, the plovers remind us of the beauty of shape, colour, and animation. They seem too slender to withstand the blast— they should have gone with the swallows—too delicate for these rude hours; yet they alone face them.

Once more the wave of rain has passed, and yonder the hills appear; these are but uplands. The nearest and highest has a green rampart, visible for a moment against the dark sky, and then again wrapped in a toga of misty cloud. So the chilled Roman drew his toga around him in ancient days as from that spot he looked wistfully southwards and thought of Italy. Wee-ah-wee! Some chance movement has been noticed by the nearest bird, and away they go at once as if with the same wings, sweeping overhead, then to the right, then to the left, and then back again, till at last lost in the coming shower. After they have thus vibrated to and fro long enough, like a pendulum coming to rest, they will alight in the open field on the ridge behind.

There in drilled ranks, well closed together, all facing the same way, they will stand for hours. Let us go also and let the shower conceal them. Another time my path leads over the hills.

It is afternoon, which in winter is evening. The sward of the down is dry under foot, but hard, and does not lift the instep with the springy feel of summer. The sky is gone, it is not clouded, it is swathed in gloom. Upwards the still air thickens, and there is no arch or vault of heaven. Formless and vague, it seems some vast shadow descending. The sun has disappeared, and the light there still is, is left in the atmosphere enclosed by the gloomy mist as pools are left by a receding tide. Through the sand the water slips, and through the mist the light glides away. Nearer comes the formless shadow, and the visible earth grows smaller. The path has faded, and there are no means on the open downs of knowing whether the direction pursued is right or wrong, till a boulder (which is a landmark) is perceived. Thence the way is down the slope, the last and limit of the hills there. It is a rough descent, the paths worn by sheep may at any moment cause a stumble. At the foot is a waggon-track beside a low hedge, enclosing the first arable field. The hedge is a guide, but the ruts are deep, and it still needs slow and careful walking. Wee-ah-wee! Up from the dusky surface of the arable field springs a plover, and the notes are immediately repeated by another. They can just be seen as darker bodies against the shadow as they fly overhead. Wee-ah-wee! The sound grows fainter as they fetch a longer circle in the gloom.

There is another winter resort of plovers in the valley where a barren waste was ploughed some years ago. A few furze bushes still stand in the hedges about it, and the corners are full of rushes. Not all the grubbing of furze and bushes, the deep ploughing and draining, has succeeded in rendering the place fertile like the adjacent fields. The character of a marsh adheres to it still. So long as there is a crop, the lapwings keep away, but as soon as the ploughs turn up the ground in autumn they return. The place lies low, and level with the waters in the ponds and streamlets. A mist hangs about it in the evening, and even when there is none, there is a distinct difference in the atmosphere while passing it. From their hereditary home the lapwings cannot be entirely driven away. Out of the mist comes their plaintive cry; they are hidden, and their exact locality is not to be discovered. Where winter rules most ruthlessly, where darkness is deepest in daylight, there the slender plovers stay undaunted.

Meadow Thoughts

THE OLD HOUSE stood by the silent country road, secluded by many a long, long mile, and yet again secluded within the great walls of the garden. Often and often I rambled up to the milestone which stood under an oak, to look at the chipped inscription low down—'To London, 79 Miles'. So far away, you see, that the very inscription was cut at the foot of the stone, since no one would be likely to want that information. It was half hidden by docks and nettles, despised and unnoticed. A broad land this seventy-nine miles—how many meadows and corn-fields, hedges and woods, in that distance?—wide enough to seclude any house, to hide it, like an acorn in the grass. Those who have lived all their lives in remote places do not feel the remoteness. No one else seemed to be conscious of the breadth that separated the place from the great centre, but it was, perhaps, that consciousness which deepened the solitude to me. It made the silence more still; the shadows of the oaks yet slower in their movement; everything more earnest. To convey a full impression of the intense concentration of Nature in the meadows is very difficult—everything is so utterly oblivious of man's thought and man's heart. The oaks stand—quiet, still—so still that the lichen loves them. At their feet the grass grows, and heeds nothing. Among it the squirrels leap, and their little hearts are as far away from you or I as the very wood of the oaks. The sunshine settles itself in the valley by the brook, and abides there whether we come or not. Glance through the gap in the hedge by the oak, and see how concentrated it is—all of it, every blade of grass, and leaf, and flower, and living creature, finch or squirrel. It is mesmerized upon itself. Then I used to feel that it really was seventy-nine miles to London, and not an hour or two only by rail, really all those miles. A great, broad province of green furrow and ploughed furrow between the old house and the city of the world. Such solace and solitude seventy-nine miles thick cannot be painted; the trees cannot be placed far enough away in perspective. It is necessary to stay in it like the oaks to know it.

Lime-tree branches overhung the corner of the garden-wall, whence a view was easy of the silent and dusty road, till overarching oaks concealed it. The white dust heated by the sunshine, the green hedges, and the heavily massed trees, white clouds rolled together in the sky, a footpath opposite lost in the fields, as you might thrust a stick into the grass, tender lime leaves caressing the cheek, and silence. That is, the silence of the fields. If a breeze rustled the boughs, if a greenfinch called, if the cart-mare in the meadow shook herself, making the earth and air tremble by her with the convulsion of her mighty muscles, these were not sounds, they were the silence itself. So sensitive to it as I was, in its turn it held me firmly, like the fabled spells of old time. The mere touch of a leaf was a talisman to bring me under the enchantment, so that I seemed to feel and know all that was proceeding among the grass-blades and in the bushes. Among the lime trees along the wall the birds never built, though so close and sheltered. They built everywhere but there. To the broad coping-stones of the wall under the lime boughs speckled thrushes came almost hourly, sometimes to peer out and reconnoitre if it was safe to visit the garden, sometimes to see if a snail had climbed up the ivy. Then they dropped quietly down into the long strawberry patch immediately under. The cover of strawberries is the constant resource of all creeping things; the thrushes looked round every plant and under every leaf and runner. One toad always resided there, often two, and as you gathered a ripe strawberry you might catch sight of his black eye watching you take the fruit he had saved for you.

Down the road skims an eave-swallow, swift as an arrow, his white back making the sun-dried dust dull and dingy; he is seeking a pool for mortar, and will waver to and fro by the brook below till he finds a convenient place to alight. Thence back to the eave here, where for forty years he and his ances-tors built in safety. Two white butterflies fluttering round each other rise over the limes, once more up over the house, and soar on till their white shows no longer against the illumined air. A grasshopper calls on the sward by the strawberries, and immediately fillips himself over seven leagues of grass-blades. Yonder a line of men and women file across the field, seen for a moment as they pass a gateway, and the hay changes from hay-colour to green behind them as they turn the under but still sappy side upwards. They are working hard, but it looks easy, slow, and sunny. Finches fly out from the hedgerow to the overturned hay. Another butterfly, a brown one, floats along the dusty road—the only traveller yet. The white clouds are slowly passing behind the oaks, large puffed clouds, like deliberate loads of hay, leaving lit-tle wisps and flecks behind them caught in the sky. How pleasant it would be to read in the shadow! There is a broad shadow on the sward by the straw-berries cast by a tall and fine-grown American crab tree. The very place for a book; and although I know it is useless, yet I go and fetch one and dispose myself on the grass.

I can never read in summer out-of-doors. Though in shadow the bright light fills it, summer shadows are broadest daylight. The page is so white and hard, the letters so very black, the meaning and drift not quite intelligible, because neither eye nor mind will dwell upon it. Human thoughts and imaginings written down are pale and feeble in bright summer light. The eye wanders away, and rests more lovingly on greensward and green lime leaves. The mind wanders yet deeper and farther into the dreamy mystery of the azure sky. Once now and then, determined to write down that mystery and delicious sense while actually in it, I have brought out table and ink and paper, and sat there in the midst of the summer day. Three words, and where is the thought? Gone. The paper is so obviously paper, the ink so evidently ink, the pen so stiff; all so inadequate. You want colour, flexibility, light, sweet low sound—all these to paint it and play it in music, at the same time you want something that will answer to and record in one touch the strong throb of life and the thought, or feeling, or whatever it is that goes out into the earth and sky and space, endless as a beam of light. The very shade of the pen on the paper tells you how utterly hopeless it is to express these things. There is the shade and the brilliant gleaming whiteness; now tell me in plain written words the simple contrast of the two. Not in twenty pages, for the bright light shows the paper in its common fibre-ground, coarse aspect, in its reality, not as a mind-tablet.

The delicacy and beauty of thought or feeling is so extreme that it cannot be inked in; it is like the green and blue of field and sky, of veronica flower and grass-blade, which in their own existence throw light and beauty on each other, but in artificial colours repel. Take the table indoors again, and the book; the thoughts and imaginings of others are vain, and of your own too deep to be written. For the mind is filled with the exceeding beauty of these things, and their great wondrousness and marvel. Never yet have I been able to write what I felt about the sunlight only. Colour and form and light are as magic to me. It is a trance. It requires a language of ideas to convey it. It is ten years since I last reclined on that grass plot, and yet I have been writing of it as if it was yesterday, and every blade of grass is as visible and as real to me now as then. They were greener towards the house, and more brown-tinted on the margin of the strawberry bed, because towards the house the shadow rested longest. By the strawberries the fierce sunlight burned them.

The sunlight put out the books I brought into it just as it put out the fire on the hearth indoors. The tawny flames floating upwards could not bite the crackling sticks when the full beams came pouring on them. Such extravagance of light overcame the little fire till it was screened from the power of the heavens. So here in the shadow of the American crab tree the light of the sky put out the written pages. For this beautiful and wonderful light excited a sense of some likewise beautiful and wonderful truth, some unknown but grand thought hovering as a swallow above. The swallows hovered and did not alight, but they were there. An inexpressible thought quivered in the azure overhead; it could not be fully grasped, but there was a sense and feeling of its presence. Before that mere sense of its presence the weak and feeble pages, the small fires of human knowledge, dwindled and lost meaning. There was something here that was not in the books. In all the philosophies and searches of mind there was nothing that could be brought to face it, to say, This is what it intends, this is the explanation of the dream. The very grass-blades confounded the wisest, the tender lime leaf put them to shame, the grasshopper derided them, the sparrow on the wall chirped his scorn. The books were put out, unless a screen were placed between them and the light of the sky—that is, an assumption, so as to make an artificial mental darkness. Grant some assumptions—that is, screen off the light—and in that darkness everything was easily arranged, this thing here, and that yonder. But nature grants no assumptions, and the books were put out. There is something beyond the philosophies in the light, in the grass-blades, the leaf, the grasshopper, the sparrow on the wall. Some day the great and beautiful thought which hovers on the confines of the mind will at last alight. In that is hope, the whole sky is full of abounding hope. Something beyond the books, that is consolation.

The little lawn beside the strawberry bed, burned brown there, and green towards the house shadow, holds how many myriad grass-blades? Here they are all matted together, long, and dragging each other down. Part them, and beneath them are still more, overhung and hidden. The fibres are intertangled, woven in an endless basket-work and chaos of green and dried threads. A blamable profusion this; a fifth as many would be enough; altogether a wilful waste here. As for these insects that spring out of it as I press the grass, a hundredth part of them would suffice. The American crab tree is a snowy mount in spring; the flakes of bloom, when they fall, cover the grass with a film—a bushel of bloom, which the wind takes and scatters afar. The extravagance is sublime. The two little cherry trees are as wasteful; they throw away handfuls of flower; but in the meadows the careless, spendthrift ways of grass and flower and all things are not to be expressed. Seeds by the hundred million float with absolute indifference on the air. The oak has a hundred thousand more leaves than necessary, and never hides a single acorn. Nothing utilitarian—everything on a scale of splendid waste. Such noble, broadcast, open-armed waste is delicious to behold. Never was there such a lying proverb as "Enough is as good as a feast." Give me the feast; give me squandered millions of seeds, luxurious carpets of petals, green mountains of oak leaves. The greater the waste, the greater the enjoyment—the nearer the approach to real life. Casuistry is of no avail; the fact is obvious; Nature flings treasures abroad, puffs them with open lips along on every breeze, piles up lavish layers of them in the free open air, packs countless numbers together in the needles of a fir tree. Prodigality and superfluity are stamped on everything she does. The ear of wheat returns a hundredfold the grain from which it grew. The surface of the earth offers to us far more than we can consume—the grains, the seeds, the fruits, the animals, the abounding products are beyond the power of all the human race to devour. They can, too, be multiplied a thousandfold. There is no natural lack. Whenever there is lack among us it is from artificial causes, which intelligence should remove.

From the littleness, and meanness, and niggardliness forced upon us by circumstances, what a relief to turn aside to the exceeding plenty of Nature! There are no bounds to it, there is no comparison to parallel it, so great is this generosity. No physical reason exists why every human being should not have sufficient, at least, of necessities. For any human being to starve, or even to be in trouble about the procuring of simple food, appears, indeed, a strange and unaccountable thing, quite upside down, and contrary to sense, if you do but consider a moment the enormous profusion the earth throws at our feet. In the slow process of time, as the human heart grows larger, such provision, I sincerely trust, will be made that no one need ever feel anxiety about mere subsistence. Then, too, let there be some imitation of this open-handed generosity and divine waste. Let the generations to come feast free of care, like my finches on the seeds of the mowing-grass, from which no voice drives them. If I could but give away as freely as the earth does!

The white-backed eave-swallow has returned many, many times from the shallow drinking-place by the brook to his half-built nest. Sometimes the pair of them cling to the mortar they have fixed under the eave, and twitter to each other about the progress of the work. They dive downwards with such veloc-ity when they quit hold that it seems as if they must strike the ground, but they shoot up again, over the wall and the lime trees. A thrush has been to the arbour yonder twenty times; it is made of crossed laths, and overgrown with 'tea-plant', and the nest is inside the lathwork. A sparrow has visited the rose tree by the wall—the buds are covered with aphides. A brown tree-creeper has been to the limes, then to the cherries, and even to a stout lilac stem. No mat-ter how small the tree, he tries all that are in his way. The bright colours of a bullfinch were visible a moment just now, as he passed across the shadows far-ther down the garden under the damson trees and into the bushes. The grasshopper has gone past and along the garden path, his voice is not heard now; but there is another coming. While I have been dreaming, all these and hundreds out in the meadow have been intensely happy. So concentrated on their little work in the sunshine, so intent on the tiny egg, on the insect cap-tured on the grass-tip to be carried to the eager fledglings, so joyful in listen-ing to the song poured out for them or in pouring it forth, quite oblivious of all else. It is in this intense concentration that they are so happy. If they could only live longer!—but a few such seasons for them—I wish they could live a hundred years just to feast on the seeds and sing and be utterly happy and oblivious of everything but the moment they are passing. A black line has rushed up from the espalier apple yonder to the housetop thirty times at least. The starlings fly so swiftly and so straight that they seem to leave a black line along the air. They have a nest in the roof, they are to and fro it and the meadow the entire day, from dawn till eve. The espalier apple, like a screen, hides the meadow from me, so that the descending starlings appear to dive into a space behind it. Sloping downwards the meadow makes a valley; I can-not see it, but know that it is golden with buttercups, and that a brook runs in the groove of it.

Afar yonder I can see a summit beyond where the grass swells upwards to a higher level than this spot. There are bushes and elms whose height is decreased by distance on the summit, horses in the shadow of the trees, and a small flock of sheep crowded, as is their wont, in the hot and sunny gate-way. By the side of the summit is a deep green trench, so it looks from here, in the hill-side: it is really the course of a streamlet worn deep in the earth. I can see nothing between the top of the espalier screen and the horses under the elms on the hill. But the starlings go up and down into the hollow space, which is aglow with golden buttercups, and, indeed, I am looking over a hundred finches eagerly searching, sweetly calling, happy as the summer day. A thousand thousand grasshoppers are leaping, thrushes are labouring, filled with love and tenderness, doves cooing—there is as much joy as there are leaves on the hedges. Faster than the starling's flight my mind runs up to the streamlet in the deep green trench beside the hill.

Pleasant it was to trace it upwards, narrowing at every ascending step, till the thin stream, thinner than fragile glass, did but merely slip over the stones. A little less and it could not have run at all, water could not stretch out to greater tenuity. It smoothed the brown growth on the stones, stroking it softly. It filled up tiny basins of sand, and ran out at the edges between minute rocks of flint. Beneath it went under thickest brooklime, blue flowered, and serrated water-parsnips, lost like many a mighty river for awhile among a forest of leaves. Higher up masses of bramble and projecting thorn stopped the explorer, who must wind round the grassy mound. Pausing to look back a moment there were meads under the hill with the shortest and greenest herbage, perpetually watered, and without one single buttercup, a strip of pure green among yellow flowers and yellowing corn. A few hollow oaks on whose boughs the cuckoos stayed to call, two or three peewits coursing up and down, larks singing, and for all else silence. Between the wheat and the grassy mound the path was almost closed, burdocks and brambles thrust the adventurer outward to brush against the wheat-ears. Upwards till suddenly it turned, and led by steep notches in the bank, as it seemed down to the roots of the elm trees. The clump of elms grew right over a deep and rugged hollow; their branches reached out across it, roofing in the cave.

Here was the spring, at the foot of a perpendicular rock, moss-grown low down, and overrun with creeping ivy higher. Green thorn bushes filled the chinks and made a wall to the well, and the long narrow hart's-tongue streaked the face of the cliff. Behind the thick thorns hid the course of the streamlet, in front rose the solid rock, upon the right hand the sward came to the edge—it shook every now and then as the horses in the shade of the elms stamped their feet—on the left hand the ears of wheat peered over the verge. A rocky cell in concentrated silence of green things. Now and again a finch, a starling, or a sparrow would come meaning to drink—athirst from the meadow or the corn-field—and start and almost entangle their wings in the bushes, so completely astonished that any one should be there. The spring rises in a hollow under the rock imperceptibly, and without bubble or sound. The fine sand of the shallow basin is undisturbed—no tiny water-volcano pushes up a dome of particles. Nor is there any crevice in the stone, but the basin is always full and always running over. As it slips from the brim a gleam of sunshine falls through the boughs and meets it. To this cell I used to come once now and then on a summer's day, tempted, perhaps, like the finches, by the sweet cool water, but drawn also by a feeling that could not be analysed. Stooping, I lifted the water in the hollow of my hand—carefully, lest the sand might be disturbed—and the sunlight gleamed on it as it slipped through my fingers. Alone in the green-roofed cave, alone with the sunlight and the pure water, there was a sense of something more than these. The water was more to me than water, and the sun than sun. The gleaming rays on the water in my palm held me for a moment, the touch of the water gave me something from itself. A moment, and the gleam was gone, the water flowing away, but I had had them. Beside the physical water and physical light I had received from them their beauty; they had communicated to me this silent mystery. The pure and beautiful water, the pure, clear, and beautiful light, each had given me something of their truth.

So many times I came to it, toiling up the long and shadowless hill in the burning sunshine, often carrying a vessel to take some of it home with me. There was a brook, indeed; but this was different, it was the spring; it was taken home as a beautiful flower might be brought. It is not the physical water, it is the sense or feeling that it conveys. Nor is it the physical sunshine; it is the sense of inexpressible beauty which it brings with it. Of such I still drink, and hope to do so still deeper.

The Sun and the Brook

THE SUN first sees the brook in the meadow where some roach swim under a bulging root of ash. Leaning against the tree, and looking down into the water, there is a picture of the sky. Its brightness hides the sandy floor of the stream as a picture conceals the wall where it hangs, but, as if the water cooled the rays, the eye can bear to gaze on the image of the sun. Over its circle thin threads of summer cloud are drawn; it is only the reflection, yet the sun seems closer seen in the brook, more to do with us, like the grass, and the tree, and the flowing stream. In the sky it is so far, it cannot be approached, nor even gazed at, so that by the very virtue and power of its own brilliance it forces us to ignore, and almost forget it. The summer days go on, and no one notices the sun. The sweet water slipping past the green flags, with every now and then a rushing sound of eager haste, receives the sky, and it becomes a part of the earth and of life. No one can see his own face without a glass; no one can sit down and deliberately think of the soul till it appears a visible thing. It eludes—the mind cannot grasp it. But hold a flower in the hand— a rose, this later honeysuckle, or this the first hare-bell—and in its beauty you can recognize your own soul reflected as the sun in the brook. For the soul finds itself in beautiful things.

Between the bulging root and the bank there is a tiny oval pool, on the surface of which the light does not fall. There the eye can see deep down into the stream, which scarcely moves in the hollow it has worn for itself as its weight swings into the concave of the bend. The hollow is illumined by the light which sinks through the stream outside the root; and beneath, in the green depth, five or six roach face the current. Every now and then a tiny curl appears on the surface inside the root, and must rise up to come there. Unwinding as it goes, its raised edge lowers and becomes lost in the level. Dark moss on the base of the ash darkens the water under. The light green leaves overhead yield gently to the passing air; there are but few leaves on the tree, and these scarcely make a shadow on the grass beyond that of the trunk. As the branch swings, the gnats are driven farther away to avoid it. Over the verge of the bank, bending down almost to the root in the water, droop the heavily seeded heads of tall grasses which, growing there, have escaped the scythe.

These are the days of the convolvulus, of ripening berry, and dropping nut. In the gateways, ears of wheat hang from the hawthorn boughs, which seized them from the passing load. The broad aftermath is without flowers; the flowers are gone to the uplands and the untilled wastes. Curving opposite the south, the hollow side of the brook has received the sunlight like a silvered speculum every day that the sun has shone. Since the first violet of the meadow, till now that the berries are ripening, through all the long drama of the summer, the rays have visited the stream. The long, loving touch of the sun has left some of its own mystic attraction in the brook. Resting here, and gazing down into it, thoughts and dreams come flowing as the water flows. Thoughts without words, mobile like the stream, nothing compact that can be grasped and stayed: dreams that slip silently as water slips through the fingers. The grass is not grass alone; the leaves of the ash above are not leaves only. From tree, and earth, and soft air moving, there comes an invisible touch which arranges the senses to its waves as the ripples of the lake set the sand in parallel lines. The grass sways and fans the reposing mind; the leaves sway and stroke it, till it can feel beyond itself and with them, using each grass blade, each leaf, to abstract life from earth and ether. These then become new organs, fresh nerves and veins running afar out into the field, along the winding brook, up through the leaves, bringing a larger existence. The arms of the mind open wide to the broad sky.

Some sense of the meaning of the grass, and leaves of the tree, and sweet waters hovers on the confines of thought, and seems ready to be resolved into definite form. There is a meaning in these things, a meaning in all that exists, and it comes near to declare itself. Not yet, not fully, nor in such shape that it may be formulated—if ever it will be—but sufficiently so to leave, as it were, an unwritten impression that will remain when the glamour is gone, and grass is but grass, and a tree a tree.

Red Roofs of London

TILES AND TILE ROOFS have a curious way of tumbling to pieces in
an irregular and eye-pleasing manner. The roof-tree bends, bows a little
under the weight, curves in, and yet preserves a sharpness at each end. The
Chinese exaggerate this curve of set purpose. Our English curve is softer,
being the product of time, which always works in true taste. The mystery of
tile-laying is not known to everyone; for to all appearance tiles seem to be put
on over a thin bed of hay or hay-like stuff. Lately they have begun to use some
sort of tarpaulin or a coarse material of that kind; but the old tiles, I fancy,
were comfortably placed on a shakedown of hay. When one slips off, little bits
of hay stick up; and to these the sparrows come, removing it bit by bit to line
their nests. If they can find a gap they get in, and a fresh couple is started in
life. By-and-by a chimney is overthrown during a twist of the wind, and half
a dozen tiles are shattered. Time passes; and at last the tiler arrives to mend
the mischief. His labour leaves a light red patch on the dark dull red of the
breadth about it. After another while the leaks along the ridge need plaster-
ing: mortar is laid on to stay the inroad of wet, adding a dull white and forming a rough, uncertain undulation along the general drooping curve. Yellow
edgings of straw project under the eaves—the work of the sparrows. A cluster
of blue-tinted pigeons gathers about the chimneyside; the smoke that comes
out of the stack droops and floats sideways, downwards, as if the chimney
enjoyed the smother as a man enjoys his pipe. Shattered here and cracked
yonder, some missing, some overlapping in curves, the tiles have an aspect of
irregular existence. They are not fixed, like slates, as it were for ever: they have
a newness, and then a middle-age, and a time of decay like human beings.

One roof is not much; but it is often a study. Put a thousand roofs, say
rather thousands of red-tiled roofs, and overlook them—not at a great alti-
tude, but at a pleasant easy angle—and then you have the groundwork of the
first view of London over Bermondsey from the railway. I say groundwork,
because the roofs seem the level and surface of the earth, while the glimpses
of streets are glimpses of catacombs. A city—as something to look at—
depends very much on its roofs. If a city have no character in its roofs it stirs
neither heart nor thought. These red-tiled roofs of Bermondsey, stretching
away mile upon mile, and brought up at the extremity with thin masts rising

above the mist—these red-tiled roofs have a distinctiveness, a character; they are something to think about. Nowhere else is there an entrance to a city like this. The roads by which you approach them give you distant aspects—minarets, perhaps, in the East, domes in Italy; but, coming nearer, the highway somehow plunges into houses, confounding you with façades, and the real place is hidden. Here from the railway you see at once the vastness of London. Roof-tree behind roof-tree, ridge behind ridge, is drawn along in succession, line behind line till they become as close together as the test-lines used for microscopes. Under this surface of roofs what a profundity of life there is! Just as the great horses in the waggons of London streets convey the idea of strength, so the endlessness of the view conveys the idea of a mass of life. Life converges from every quarter. The iron way has many ruts: the rails are its ruts; and by each of these a ceaseless stream of men and women pours over the tiled roofs into London. They come from the populous suburbs, from far-away towns and quiet villages, and from over sea.

Glance down as you pass into the excavations, the streets, beneath the red surface: you catch a glimpse of men and women hastening to and fro, of vehicles, of horses struggling with mighty loads, of groups at the corners, and fragments, as it were, of crowds. Busy life everywhere: no stillness, no quiet, no repose. Life crowded and crushed together; life that has hardly room to live. If the train slackens, look in at the open windows of the houses level with the line—they are always open for air, smoke-laden as it is—and see women and children with scarce room to move, the bed and the dining-table in the same apartment. For they dine and sleep and work and play all at the same time. A man works at night and sleeps by day: he lies yonder as calmly as if in a quiet country cottage. The children have no place to play in but the living-room or the street. It is not squalor—it is crowded life. The people are pushed together by the necessities of existence. These people have no dislike to it at all: it is right enough to them, and so long as business is brisk they are happy. The man who lies sleeping so calmly seems to me to indicate the immensity of the life around more than all the rest. He is oblivious of it all; it does not make him nervous or wakeful; he is so used to it, and bred to it, that it seems to him nothing. When he is awake he does not see it; now he sleeps he does not hear it. It is only in great woods that you cannot see the trees. He is like a leaf in a forest—he is not conscious of it. Long hours of work have given him slumber; and as he sleeps he seems to express by contrast the immensity and endlessness of the life around him.

Sometimes a floating haze, now thicker here, and now lit up yonder by the sunshine, brings out objects more distinctly than a clear atmosphere. Away there tall thin masts stand out, rising straight up above the red roofs. There is a faint colour on them; the yards are dark—being inclined, they do not reflect the light at an angle to reach us. Half-furled canvas droops in folds, now swelling a little as the wind blows, now heavily sinking. One white sail is set and gleams alone among the dusky folds; for the canvas at large is dark with coal-dust, with smoke, with the grime that settles everywhere where men labour with bare arms and chests. Still and quiet as trees the masts rise into the hazy air; who would think, merely to look at them, of the endless labour they mean? The labour to load, and the labour to unload; the labour at sea, and the long hours of ploughing the waves by night; the labour at the warehouses; the labour in the fields, the mines, the mountains; the labour in the factories. Ever and again the sunshine gleams now on this group of masts, now on that; for they stand in groups as trees often grow, a thicket here and a thicket yonder. Labour to obtain the material, labour to bring it hither, labour to force it into shape—work without end. Masts are always dreamy to look at: they speak a romance of the sea; of unknown lands; of distant forests aglow with tropical colours and abounding with strange forms of life. In the hearts of most of us there is always a desire for something beyond experience. Hardly any of us but have thought, Some day I will go on a long voyage; but the years go by, and still we have not sailed.

Wild Flowers

A FIR-TREE is not a flower, and yet it is associated in my mind with prim-roses. There was a narrow lane leading into a wood, where I used to go almost every day in the early months of the year, and at one corner it was overlooked by three spruce firs. The rugged lane there began to ascend the hill, and I paused a moment to look back. Immediately the high fir-trees guided the eye upwards, and from their tops to the deep azure of the March sky over, but a step from the tree to the heavens. So it has ever been to me, by day or by night, summer or winter, beneath trees the heart feels nearer to that depth of life the far sky means. The rest of spirit found only in beauty, ideal and pure, comes there because the distance seems within the touch of thought. To the heaven thought can reach lifted by the strong arms of the oak, carried up by the ascent of the flame-shaped fir. Round the spruce top the blue was deepened, concentrated by the fixed point; the memory of that spot, as it were, of the sky is still fresh—I can see it distinctly—still beautiful and full of meaning. It is painted in bright colour in my mind, colour thrice laid, and indelible; as one passes a shrine and bows the head to the Madonna, so I recall the picture and stoop in spirit to the aspiration it yet arouses. For there is no saint like the sky, sunlight shining from its face.

The fir-tree flowered thus before the primroses—the first of all to give me a bloom, beyond reach but visible, while even the hawthorn buds hesitated to open. Primroses were late there, a high district and thin soil; you could read of them as found elsewhere in January; they rarely came much before March, and but sparingly then. On the warm red sand (red at least, to look at, but green by geological courtesy, I think) of Sussex, round about Hurst of the Pierrepoints, primroses are seen soon after the year has turned. In the lanes about that curious old mansion, with its windows reaching from floor to roof, that stands at the base of Wolstanbury Hill, they grow early, and ferns linger in sheltered overhung banks. The South Down range, like a great wall, shuts off the sea, and has a different climate on either hand; south by the sea—hard, harsh, flowerless, almost grassless, bitter, and cold; on the north side, just over the hill—warm, soft, with primroses and fern, willows budding and birds already busy. It is a double England there, two countries side by side.

On a summer's day Wolstanbury Hill is an island in sunshine; you may lie on the grassy rampart, high up in the most delicate air—Grecian air, pellucid—alone, among the butterflies and humming bees at the thyme, alone and isolated; endless masses of hills on three sides, endless weald or valley on the fourth; all warmly lit with sunshine, deep under liquid sunshine like the sands under the liquid sea, no harshness of man-made sound to break the insulation amid nature, on an island in a far Pacific of sunshine. Some people would hesitate to walk down the staircase cut in the turf to the beech trees beneath; the woods look so small beneath, so far down and steep, and no handrail. Many go to the Dyke, but none to Wolstanbury Hill. To come over the range reminds one of what travellers say of coming over the Alps into Italy; from harsh sea-slopes, made dry with salt as they sow salt on razed cities that naught may grow, to warm plains rich in all things, and with great hills as pictures hung on a wall to gaze at. Where there are beech-trees the land is always beautiful; beech-trees at the foot of this hill, beech-trees at Arundel in that lovely park which the Duke of Norfolk, to his glory, leaves open to all the world, and where the anemones flourish in unusual size and number; beech-trees in Marlborough Forest; beech-trees at the summit to which the lane leads that was spoken of just now. Beech and beautiful scenery go together.

But the primroses by that lane did not appear till late; they covered the banks under the thousand thousand ashpoles; foxes slipped along there frequently, whose friends in scarlet coats could not endure the pale flowers, for they might chink their spurs homewards. In one meadow near primroses were thicker than the grass, with gorse interspersed, and the rabbits that came out fed among flowers. The primroses last on to the celandines and cowslips, through the time of the bluebells, past the violets—one dies but passes on the life to another, one sets light to the next, till the ruddy oaks and singing cuckoos call up the tall mowing grass to fringe summer.

Before I had any conscious thought it was a delight to me to find wild flowers, just to see them. It was a pleasure to gather them and to take them home; a pleasure to show them to others—to keep them as long as they would live, to decorate the room with them, to arrange them carelessly with grasses, green sprays, tree-bloom—large branches of chestnut snapped off, and set by a picture perhaps. Without conscious thought of seasons and the advancing hours to light on the white wild violet, the meadow orchis, the blue veronica, the blue meadow cranesbill; feeling the warmth and delight of the increasing sun-rays, but not recognizing whence or why it was joy. All the world is young to a boy, and thought has not entered into it; even the old men with grey hair do not seem old; different but not aged, the idea of age has not been mastered. A boy has to frown and study, and then does not grasp what long years mean.

The various hues of the petals pleased without any knowledge of colour-contrasts, no note even of colour except that it was bright, and the mind was made happy without consideration of those ideals and hopes afterwards associated with the azure sky above the fir-tree. A fresh footpath, a fresh flower, a fresh delight. The reeds, the grasses, the rushes—unknown and new things at every step—something always to find; no barren spot anywhere, or sameness. Every day the grass painted anew, and its green seen for the first time; not the old green, but a novel hue and spectacle, like the first view of the sea.

If we had never before looked upon the earth, but suddenly came to it man or woman grown, set down in the midst of a summer mead, would it not seem to us a radiant vision? The hues, the shapes, the song and life of birds, above all the sunlight, the breath of heaven, resting on it; the mind would be filled with its glory, unable to grasp it, hardly believing that such things could be mere matter and no more. Like a dream of some spirit-land it would appear, scarce fit to be touched lest it should fall to pieces, too beautiful to be long watched lest it should fade away. So it seemed to me as a boy, sweet and new like this each morning; and even now, after the years that have passed, and the lines they have worn in the forehead, the summer mead shines as bright and fresh as when my foot first touched the grass. It has another meaning now; the sunshine and the flowers speak differently, for a heart that has once known sorrow reads behind the page, and sees sadness in joy. But the freshness is still there, the dew washes the colours before dawn. Unconscious happiness in finding wild flowers—unconscious and unquestioning, and therefore unbounded.

I used to stand by the mower and follow the scythe sweeping down thousands of the broad-flowered daisies, the knotted knapweeds, the blue scabious, the yellow rattles, sweeping so close and true that nothing escaped; and yet, although I had seen so many hundreds of each, although I had lifted armfuls day after day, still they were fresh. They never lost their newness, and even now each time I gather a wild flower it feels a new thing. The greenfinches came to the fallen swathe so near to us they seemed to have no fear; but I remember the yellowhammers most, whose colour, like that of the wild flowers and the sky, has never faded from my memory. The greenfinches sank into the fallen swathe, the loose grass gave under their weight and let them bathe in flowers.

One yellowhammer sat on a branch of ash the livelong morning, still singing in the sun; his bright head, his clean bright yellow, gaudy as Spain, was drawn like a brush charged heavily with colour across the retina, painting it deeply, for there on the eye's memory it endures, though that was boyhood and this is manhood, still unchanged. The field—Stewart's Mash— the very tree, young ash timber, the branch projecting over the sward, I could make a map of them. Sometimes I think sun-painted colours are brighter to me than to many, and more strongly affect the nerves of the eye. Straw going by the road on a dusky winter's day seems so pleasantly golden, the sheaves lying aslant at the top, and these bundles of yellow tubes thrown up against the dark ivy on the opposite wall. Tiles, red burned, or orange coated, the sea sometimes cleanly definite, the shadows of trees in a thin wood where there is room for shadows to form and fall; some such shadows are sharper than light, and have a faint blue tint. Not only in summer but in cold winter, and not only romantic things but plain matter-of-fact things as a wagon freshly painted red beside the wright's shop, stand out as if wet with colour and delicately pencilled at the edges. It must be out of doors; nothing indoors looks like this.

Pictures are very dull and gloomy to it, and very contrasted colours like those the French use are necessary to fix the attention. Their dashes of pink and scarlet bring the faint shadow of the sun into the room. As for our painters, their works are hung behind a curtain, and we have to peer patiently through the dusk of evening to see what they mean. Out-of-door colours do not need to be gaudy—a mere dull stake of wood thrust in the ground often stands out sharper than the pink flashes of the French studio; a faggot; the outline of a leaf; low tints without reflecting power strike the eye as a bell the ear. To me they are intensely clear, and the clearer the greater the pleasure. It is often too great, for it takes me away from solid pursuits merely to receive the impression, as water is still to reflect the trees. To me it is very painful when illness blots the definition of outdoor things, so wearisome not to see them rightly, and more oppressive than actual pain. I feel as if I was struggling to wake up with dim, half-opened lids and heavy mind. This one yellow-hammer still sits on the ash branch in Stewart's Mash over the sward, singing in the sun, his feathers freshly wet with colour, the same sun-song, and will sing to me so long as the heart shall beat.

The first conscious thought about wild flowers was to find out their names—the first conscious pleasure,—and then I began to see so many that I had not previously noticed. Once you wish to identify them there is nothing escapes, down to the little white chickweed of the path and the moss of the wall. I put my hand on the bridge across the brook to lean over and look down into the water. Are there any fish? The bricks of the pier are covered with green, like a wall-painting to the surface of the stream, mosses along the lines of the mortar, and among the moss little plants—what are these? In the dry sunlit lane I look up to the top of the great wall about some domain, where the green figs look over upright on their stalks; there are dry plants on the coping—what are these? Some growing thus, high in the air, on stone, and in the chinks of the tower, suspended in dry air and sunshine; some low down under the arch of the bridge over the brook, out of sight utterly, unless you stoop by the brink of the water and project yourself forward to examine under. The kingfisher sees them as he shoots through the barrel of the culvert. There the sun direct never shines upon them, but the sunlight thrown up by the ripples runs all day in bright bars along the vault of the arch, playing on them. The stream arranges the sand in the shallow in bars, minute fixed undulations; the stream arranges the sunshine in successive flashes, undulating as if the sun, drowsy in the heat, were idly closing and unclosing his eyelids for sleep. Plants everywhere, hiding behind every tree, under the leaves, in the shady places, beside the dry furrows of the field; they are only just behind something, hidden openly. The instant you look for them they multiply a hundredfold; if you sit on the beach and begin to count the pebbles by you, their number instantly increases to infinity by virtue of that conscious act.

The bird's-foot lotus was the first. The boy must have seen it, must have trodden on it in the bare woodland pastures, certainly run about on it, with wet naked feet from the bathing; but the boy was not conscious of it. This was the first, when the desire came to identify and to know, fixing upon it by means of a pale and feeble picture. In the largest pasture there were different soils and climates; it was so large it seemed a little country of itself then—the more so because the ground rose and fell, making a ridge to divide the view and enlarge by uncertainty. The high sandy soil on the ridge where the rabbits had their warren; the rocky soil of the quarry; the long grass by the elms where the rooks built, under whose nests there were vast unpalatable mushrooms— the true mushrooms with salmon gills grew nearer the warren; the slope towards the nut-tree hedge and spring. Several climates in one field: the wintry ridge over which leaves were always driving in all four seasons of the year; the level sunny plain and fallen cromlech still tall enough for a gnomon and to cast its shadow in the treeless drought; the moist, warm, grassy depression; the lotus-grown slope, warm and dry.

If you have been living in one house in the country for some time, and then go on a visit to another though hardly half a mile distant, you will find a change in the air, the feeling, and tone of the place. It is close by, but it is not the same. To discover these minute differences, which make one locality healthy and home happy, and the next adjoining unhealthy, the Chinese have invented the science of Feng-shui, spying about with cabalistic mystery, casting the horoscope of an acre. There is something in all superstitions; they are often the foundation of science. Superstition having made the discovery, science composes a lecture on the reason why, and claims the credit. Bird's-foot lotus means a fortunate spot, dry, warm—so far as soil is concerned. If you were going to live out of doors, you might safely build your kibitka where you found it. Wandering with the pictured flower-book, just purchased, over the windy ridge where last year's skeleton leaves, blown out from the alder copse below, came on with grasshopper motion—lifted and laid down by the wind, lifted and laid down—I sat on the sward of the sheltered slope, and instantly recognized the orange-red claws of the flower beside me. That was the first; and this very morning, I dread to consider how many years afterwards, I found a plant on a wall which I do not know. I shall have to trace out its genealogy and emblazon its shield. So many years and still only at the beginning—the beginning, too, of the beginning—for as yet I have not thought of the garden or conservatory flowers (which are wild flowers somewhere), or of the tropics, or the prairies.

The great stone of the fallen cromlech, crouching down afar off in the plain behind me, cast its shadow in the sunny morn as it had done, so many summers, for centuries—for thousands of years: worn white by the endless sunbeams—ceaseless flood of light—the sunbeams of centuries, the impalpable beams polishing and grinding like rushing water; silent, yet witnessing of the Past; shadowing the Present on the dial of the field: a mere dull stone; but what is it the mind will not employ to express to itself its own thoughts?

There was a hollow near in which hundreds of skeleton leaves had settled, a stage on their journey from the alder copse, so thick as to cover the thin grass, and at the side of the hollow a wasp's nest had been torn out by a badger. On the soft and spreading sand thrown out from his burrow the print of his foot looked as large as an elephant might make. The wild animals of our fields are so small that the badger's foot seemed foreign in its size, calling up the thought of the great game of distant forests. He was a bold badger to make his burrow there in the open warren, unprotected by park walls or preserve laws, where everyone might see who chose. I never saw him by daylight: that they do get about in daytime is, however, certain, for one was shot in Surrey recently by sportsmen; they say he weighed forty pounds.

In the mind all things are written in pictures—there is no alphabetical combination of letters and words; all things are pictures and symbols. The bird's-foot lotus is the picture to me of sunshine and summer, and of that summer in the heart which is known only in youth, and then not alone. No words could write that feeling: the bird's-foot lotus writes it.

When the efforts to photograph began, the difficulty was to fix the scene thrown by the lens upon the plate. There the view appeared perfect to the least of details, worked out by the sun, and made as complete in miniature as that he shone upon in nature. But it faded like the shadows as the summer sun declines. Have you watched them in the fields among the flowers?—the deep strong mark of the noonday shadow of a tree such as the pen makes drawn heavily on the paper; gradually it loses its darkness and becomes paler and thinner at the edge as it lengthens and spreads, till shadow and grass mingle together. Image after image faded from the plates, no more to be fixed than the reflection in water of the trees by the shore. Memory, like the sun, paints to me bright pictures of the golden summer time of lotus; I can see them, but how shall I fix them for you? By no process can that be accomplished. It is like a story that cannot be told because he who knows it is tongue-tied and dumb. Motions of hands, wavings and gestures, rudely convey the framework, but the finish is not there.

To-day, and day after day, fresh pictures are coloured instantaneously in the retina as bright and perfect in detail and hue. This very power is often, I think, the cause of pain to me. To see so clearly is to value so highly and to feel too deeply. The smallest of the pencilled branches of the bare ash-tree drawn distinctly against the winter sky, waving lines one within the other, yet following and partly parallel, reproducing in the curve of the twig the curve of the great trunk; is it not a pleasure to trace each to its ending? The raindrops as they slide from leaf to leaf in June, the balmy shower that reperfumes each wild flower and green thing, drops lit with the sun, and falling to the chorus of the refreshed birds; is not this beautiful to see? On the grasses tall and heavy the purplish blue pollen, a shimmering dust, sown broadcast over the ripening meadow from July's warm hand—the bluish pollen, the lilac pollen of the grasses, a delicate mist of blue floating on the surface, has always been an especial delight to me. Finches shake it from the stalks as they rise. No day, no hour of summer, no step but brings new mazes—there is no word to express design without plan, and these designs of flower and leaf and colours of the sun cannot be reduced to set order. The eye is for ever drawn onward and finds no end. To see these always so sharply, wet and fresh, is almost too much sometimes for the wearied yet insatiate eye. I am obliged to turn away—to shut my eyes and say I *will* not see, I will not observe; I will concentrate my mind on my own little path of life, and steadily gaze downwards. In vain. Who can do so? who can care alone for his or her petty trifles of existence, that has once entered amongst the wild flowers? How shall I shut out the sun? Shall I deny the constellations of the night? They are there; the Mystery is for ever about us—the question, the hope, the aspiration cannot be put out. So that it is almost a pain not to be able to cease observing and tracing the untraceable maze of beauty.

Blue veronica was the next identified, sometimes called germander speedwell, sometimes bird's-eye, whose leaves are so plain and petals so blue. Many names increase the trouble of identification, and confusion is made certain by the use of various systems of classification. The flower itself I knew, its name

I could not be sure of—not even from the illustration, which was incorrectly coloured; the central white spot of the flower was reddish in the plate. This incorrect colouring spoils much of the flower-picturing done; pictures of flowers and birds are rarely accurate unless hand-painted. Anyone else, how-ever, would have been quite satisfied that the identification was right. I was too desirous to be correct, too conscientious, and thus a summer went by with little progress. If you really wish to identify with certainty, and have no botanist friend and no *magnum opus* of Sowerby to refer to, it is very difficult indeed to be quite sure. There was no Sowerby, no Bentham, no botanist friend—no one even to give the common country names; for it is a curious fact that the country people of the time rarely know the names put down as the vernacular for flowers in the books.

No one there could tell me the name of the marsh-marigold which grew thickly in the water-meadows—'A sort of big buttercup', that was all they knew. Commonest of common plants is the 'sauce alone'—in every hedge, on every bank, the whitish-green leaf is found—yet I could not make certain of it. If someone tells you a plant, you know it at once and never forget it, but to learn it from a book is another matter; it does not at once take root in the mind, it has to be seen several times before you are satisfied—you waver in your convictions. The leaves were described as large and heart-shaped, and to remain green (at the ground) through the winter; but the colour of the flower was omitted, though it was stated that the petals of the hedge-mustard were yellow. The plant that seemed to me to be probably 'sauce alone' had leaves somewhat heart-shaped, but so confusing is *partial* description that I began to think I had hit on 'ramsons' instead of 'sauce alone', especially as ramsons was said to be a very common plant. So it is in some counties, but, as I after-wards found, there was not a plant of ramsons, or garlic, throughout the whole of that district. When, some years afterwards, I saw a white-flowered plant with leaves like the lily of the valley, smelling of garlic, in the woods of Somerset, I recognized it immediately. The plants that are really common—common everywhere—are not numerous, and if you are studying you must be careful to understand that word locally. My 'sauce alone' identification was right; to be right and not certain is still unsatisfactory.

There shone on the banks white stars among the grass. Petals delicately white in a whorl of rays—light that had started radiating from a centre and become fixed—shining among the flowerless green. The slender stem had grown so fast it had drawn its own root partly out of the ground, and when I tried to gather it, flower, stem and root came away together. The wheat was springing, the soft air full of the growth and moisture, blackbirds whistling, wood-pigeons nesting, young oak-leaves out; a sense of swelling, sunny fulness in the atmosphere. The plain road was made beautiful by the advanced boughs that overhung and cast their shadows on the dust—boughs of ash-green, shadows that lay still, listening to the nightingale. A place of enchantment in the mornings, where was felt the power of some subtle influence working behind bough and grass and bird-song. The orange-golden dandelion in the sward was deeply laden with colour brought to it anew again and again by the ships of the flowers, the humble-bees—to their quays they come, unlading priceless essences of sweet odours brought from the East over the green seas of wheat, unlading priceless colours on the broad dandelion disks, bartering these things for honey and pollen. Slowly tacking aslant, the pollen ship hums in the south wind. The little brown wren finds her way through the great thicket of hawthorn. How does she know her path, hidden by a thousand thousand leaves? Tangled and crushed together by their own growth, a crown of thorns hangs over the thrush's nest; thorns for the mother, hope for the young. Is there a crown of thorns over your heart? A spike has gone deep enough into mine. The stile looks farther away because boughs have pushed forward and made it smaller. The willow scarce holds the sap that tightens the bark and would burst it if it did not enlarge to the pressure.

Two things can go through the solid oak; the lightning of the clouds that

rends the iron timber, the lightning of the spring—the electricity of the sunbeams forcing him to stretch forth and lengthen his arms with joy. Bathed in buttercups to the dewlap, the roan cows standing in the golden lake watched the hours with calm frontlet; watched the light descending, the meadows filling, with knowledge of long months of succulent clover. On their broad brows the year falls gently; their great, beautiful eyes, which need but a tear or a smile to make them human—without these, such eyes, so large and full, seem above human life, eyes of the immortals enduring without passion—in these eyes, as a mirror, nature is reflected.

I came every day to walk slowly up and down the plain road, by the starry flowers under the ash-green boughs; ash is the coolest, softest green. The bees went drifting over by my head; as they cleared the hedges they passed by my ears, the wind singing in their shrill wings. White tent-walls of cloud—a warm white, being full to overflowing of sunshine—stretched across from ash-top to ash-top, a cloud-canvas roof, a tent-palace of the delicious air. For of all things there is none so sweet as sweet air—one great flower it is, drawn round about, over, and enclosing, like Aphrodite's arms; as if the dome of the sky were a bell-flower drooping down over us, and the magical essence of it filling all the room of the earth. Sweetest of all things is wild-flower air. Full of their ideal the starry flowers strained upwards on the bank, striving to keep above the rude grasses that pushed by them; genius has ever had such a struggle. The plain road was made beautiful by the many thoughts it gave. I came every morning to stay by the star-lit bank.

A friend said, "Why do you go the same road every day? Why not have a change and walk somewhere else sometimes? Why keep on up and down the same place?" I could not answer; till then it had not occurred to me that I did always go one way; as for the reason of it I could not tell; I continued in my old mind while the summers went away. Not till years afterwards was I able to see why I went the same round and did not care for change. I do not want change: I want the same old and loved things, the same wild flowers, the same trees and soft ash-green; the turtle-doves, the blackbirds, the coloured yellow-hammer sing, sing, singing so long as there is light to cast a shadow on the dial, for such is the measure of his song, and I want them in the same place. Let me find them morning after morning, the starrywhite petals radiating, striving upwards to their ideal. Let me see the idle shadows resting on the white dust; let me hear the humble-bees, and stay to look down on the rich dandelion disk. Let me see the very thistles opening their great crowns—I should miss the thistles; the reed-grasses hiding the moorhen; the bryony bine, at first crudely ambitious and lifted by force of youthful sap straight above the hedgerow to sink of its own weight presently and progress with crafty tendrils; swifts shot through the air with outstretched wings like crescent-headed shaftless arrows darted from the clouds; the chaffinch with a feather in her bill; all the living staircase of the spring, step by step, upwards to the great gallery of the summer—let me watch the same succession year by year.

Why, I knew the very dates of them all—the reddening elm, the arum, the hawthorn leaf, the celandine, the may; the yellow iris of the waters, the heath of the hillside. The time of the nightingale—the place to hear the first note; onwards to the drooping fern and the time of the redwing—the place of *his* first note, so welcome to the sportsman as the acorn ripens and the pheasant, come to the age of manhood, feeds himself; onwards to the shadowless days—

the long shadowless winter, for in winter it is the shadows we miss as much as the light. They lie over the summer sward, design upon design, dark lace on green and gold; they glorify the sunlight: they repose on the distant hills like gods upon Olympus; without shadow, what even is the sun? At the foot of the great cliffs by the sea you may know this, it is dry glare; mighty ocean is dearer as the shadows of the clouds sweep over as they sweep over the green corn. Past the shadowless winter, when it is all shade, and therefore no shadow; onwards to the first coltsfoot and on to the seedtime again; I knew the dates of all of them. I did not want change; I wanted the same flowers to return on the same day, the titlark to rise soaring from the same oak to fetch down love with a song from heaven to his mate on the nest beneath. No change, no new thing; if I found a fresh wild flower in a fresh place, still it wove at once into the old garland. In vain, the very next year was different even in the same place—*that* had been a year of rain, and the flag flowers were wonderful to see; *this* was a dry year, and the flags not half the height, the gold of the flower not so deep; next year the fatal billhook came and swept away a slow-grown hedge that had given me crab-blossom in cuckoo-time and hazelnuts in harvest. Never again the same, even in the same place.

A little feather droops downwards to the ground—a swallow's feather fuller of miracle than the Pentateuch—how shall that feather be placed again in the breast where it grew? Nothing twice. Time changes the places that knew us, and if we go back in after years, still even then it is not the old spot; the gate swings differently, new thatch has been put on the old gables, the road has been widened, and the sward the driven sheep lingered on is gone. Who dares to think then? For faces fade as flowers, and there is no consolation. So now I am sure I was right in always walking the same way by the starry flowers striving upwards on a slender ancestry of stem; I would follow the plain old road to-day if I could. Let change be far from me; that irresistible change must come is bitter indeed. Give me the old road, the same flowers—they were only stitchwort—the old succession of days and garland, ever weaving into it fresh wildflowers from far and near. Fetch them from distant mountains, discover them on decaying walls, in unsuspected corners; though never seen before, still they are the same; there has been a place in the heart waiting for them.

One of the New Voters

I F ANY ONE were to get up about half-past five on an August morning and look out of an eastern window in the country, he would see the distant trees almost hidden by a white mist. The tops of the larger groups of elms would appear above it, and by these the line of the hedgerows could be traced. Tier after tier they stretch along, rising by degrees on a gentle slope, the space between filled with haze. Whether there were cornfields or meadows under this white cloud he could not tell—a cloud that might have come down from the sky, leaving it a clear azure. This morning haze means intense heat in the day. It is hot already, very hot, for the sun is shining with all his strength, and if you wish the house to be cool it is time to set the sun blinds.

Roger, the reaper, had slept all night in the cowhouse, lying on the raised platform of narrow planks put up for cleanliness when the cattle were there. He had set the wooden window wide open and left the door ajar when he came stumbling in overnight, long after the late swallows had settled in their nests on the beams, and the bats had wearied of moth catching. One of the swallows twittered a little, as much as to say to his mate, 'My love, it is only a reaper, we need not be afraid,' and all was silence and darkness. Roger did not so much as take off his boots, but flung himself on the boards crash, curled himself up hedgehog fashion with some old sacks, and immediately began to breathe heavily. He had no difficulty in sleeping, first because his muscles had been tried to the utmost, and next because his skin was full to the brim, not of jolly 'good ale and old', but of the very smallest and poorest of wish-washy beer. In his own words, it 'blowed him up till he very nigh bust.' Now the great author- ities on dyspepsia, so eagerly studied by the wealthy folk whose stomachs are deranged, tell us that a very little flatulence will make the heart beat irregularly and cause the most distressing symptoms.

Roger had swallowed at least a gallon of a liquid chemically designed, one might say, on purpose to utterly upset the internal economy. Harvest beer is probably the vilest drink in the world. The men say it is made by pouring muddy water into empty casks returned sour from use, and then brushing them round and round inside with a besom. This liquid leaves a stickiness on the tongue and a harsh feeling at the back of the mouth which soon turns to thirst, so that having once drunk a pint the drinker must go on drinking. The peculiar dryness caused by this beer is not like any other throat drought—worse than dust, or heat, or thirst from work; there is no satisfying it. With it there go down the germs of fermentation, a sour, yeasty, and, as it were, secondary fermentation; not that kind which is necessary to make beer, but the kind that unmakes and spoils beer. It is beer rotting and decomposing in the stomach. Violent diarrhoea often follows, and then the exhaustion thus caused induces the men to drink more in order to regain the strength necessary to do their work. The great heat of the sun and the heat of hard labour, the strain and perspiration, of course try the body and weaken the digestion. To distend the stomach with half a gallon of this liquor, expressly compounded to ferment, is about the most murderous thing a man could do—murderous because it exposes him to the risk of sunstroke. So vile a drink there is not elsewhere in the world; arrack, and potato-spirit, and all the other killing extracts of the distiller are not equal to it. Upon this abominable mess the golden harvest of English fields is gathered in.

Some people have in consequence endeavoured to induce the harvesters to accept a money payment in place of beer, and to a certain extent successfully. Even then, however, they must drink something. Many manage on weak tea after a fashion, but not so well as the abstainers would have us think. Others have brewed for their men a miserable stuff in buckets, an infusion of oatmeal, and got a few to drink it; but English labourers will never drink oatmeal water unless they are paid to do it. If they are paid extra beer-money and oatmeal water is made for them gratis, some will, of course, imbibe it, especially if they see that thereby they may obtain little favours from their employer by yielding to his fad. By drinking the crotchet perhaps they may get a present now and then—food for themselves, cast-off clothes for their families, and so on. For it is a remarkable feature of human natural history, the desire to proselytize. The spectacle of John Bull—jovial John Bull—offering his men a bucket of oatmeal liquor is not a pleasant one. Such a John Bull ought to be ashamed of himself.

The truth is the English farmer's man was and is, and will be, a drinker of beer. Neither tea, nor oatmeal, nor vinegar and water (coolly recommended by indoor folk) will do for him. His natural constitution rebels against such 'peevish' drink. In winter he wants beer against the cold and the frosty rime and the heavy raw mist that hangs about the hollows; in spring and autumn against the rain, and in summer to support him under the pressure of additional work and prolonged hours. Those who really wish well to the labourer cannot do better than see that he really has beer to drink—real beer, genuine brew of malt and hops, a moderate quantity of which will supply force to his thews and sinews, and will not intoxicate or injure. If by giving him a small money payment in lieu of such large quantities you can induce him to be content with a little, so much the better. If an employer followed that plan, and at the same time once or twice a day sent out a moderate supply of genuine beer as a gift to his men, he would do them all the good in the world, and at the same time obtain for himself their goodwill and hearty assistance, that hearty work which is worth so much.

Roger breathed heavily in his sleep in the cowhouse, because the vile stuff he had taken puffed him up and obstructed nature. The tongue in his open mouth became parched and cracked, swollen and dry; he slept indeed, but he did not rest; he groaned heavily at times and rolled aside. Once he awoke choking—he could not swallow, his tongue was so dry and large; he sat up, swore, and again lay down. The rats in the sties had already discovered that a man slept in the cowhouse, a place they rarely visited, as there was nothing there to eat; how they found it out no one knows. They are clever creatures, the despised rats. They came across in the night and looked under his bed, supposing that he might have eaten his bread-and-cheese for supper there, and that fragments might have dropped between the boards. There were none. They mounted the boards and sniffed round him; they would have stolen the food from his very pocket if it had been there. Nor could they find a bundle in a handkerchief, which they would have gnawn through speedily. Not a scrap of food was there to be smelt at, so they left him. Roger had indeed gone supperless, as usual; his supper he had swilled and not eaten. His own fault; he should have exercised self-control. Well, I don't know; let us consider further before we judge.

In houses the difficulty often is to get the servants up in the morning; one cannot wake, and the rest sleep too sound—much the same thing; yet they have clocks and alarums. The reapers are never behind. Roger got off his planks, shook himself, went outside the shed, and tightened his shoelaces in the bright light. His rough hair he just pushed back from his forehead, and that was his toilet. His dry throat sent him to the pump, but he did not swallow much of the water—he washed his mouth out, and that was enough; and so without breakfast he went to his work. Looking down from the stile on the high ground there seemed to be a white cloud resting on the valley, through which the tops of the high trees penetrated; the hedgerows beneath were concealed, and their course could only be traced by the upper branches of the elms. Under this cloud the wheat-fields were blotted out; there seemed neither corn nor grass, work for man nor food for animal; there could be nothing doing there surely. In the stillness of the August morning, without song of bird, the sun, shining brilliantly high above the mist, seemed to be the only living thing, to possess the whole and reign above absolute peace. It is a curious sight to see the early harvest morn—all hushed under the burning sun, a morn that

you know is full of life and meaning, yet quiet as if man's foot had never trodden the land. Only the sun is there, rolling on his endless way.

Roger's head was bound with brass, but had it not been he would not have
observed anything in the aspect of the earth. Had a brazen band been drawn
firmly round his forehead, it could not have felt more stupefied. His eyes
blinked in the sunlight; every now and then he stopped to save himself from
staggering; he was not in a condition to think. It would have mattered not at
all if his head had been clear; earth, sky, and sun were nothing to him; he
knew the footpath, and saw that the day would be fine and hot, and that was
sufficient for him, because his eyes had never been opened.

The reaper had risen early to his labour, but the birds had preceded him
hours. Before the sun was up the swallows had left their beams in the
cow-shed and twittered out into the air. The rooks and wood-pigeons and
doves had gone to the corn, the blackbird to the stream, the finch to the
hedgerow, the bees to the heath on the hills, the humble-bees to the clover in
the plain. Butterflies rose from the flowers by the footpath, and fluttered
before him to and fro and round and back again to the place whence they had
been driven. Goldfinches tasting the first thistledown rose from the corner
where the thistles grew thickly. A hundred sparrows came rushing up into the
hedge, suddenly filling the boughs with brown fruit; they chirped and quar-
relled in their talk, and rushed away again back to the corn as he stepped
nearer. The boughs were stripped of their winged brown berries as quickly as
they had grown. Starlings ran before the cows feeding in the aftermath, so
close to their mouths as to seem in danger of being licked up by their broad
tongues. All creatures, from the tiniest insect upward, were in reality busy
under that curtain of white-heat haze. It looked so still, so quiet, from afar;
entering it and passing among the fields, all that lived was found busy at its
long day's work. Roger did not interest himself in these things, in the wasps
that left the gate as he approached—they were making *papier-maché* from the
wood of the top bar,—in the bright poppies brushing against his drab unpol-
ished boots, in the hue of the wheat or the white convolvulus; they were nothing to him.

Why should they be? His life was work without skill or thought, the work
of the horse, of the crane that lifts stone and timber. His food was rough, his
drink rougher, his lodging dry planks. His books were—none; his
picture-gallery a coloured print at the alehouse—a dog, dead, by a barrel,
'Trust is dead; Bad Pay killed him.' Of thought he thought nothing; of hope
his idea was a shilling a week more wages; of any future for himself of comfort such as even a good cottage can give—of any future whatever—he had
no more conception than the horse in the shafts of the waggon. A human ani-

mal simply in all this, yet if you reckoned upon him as simply an animal—as has been done these centuries—you would now be mistaken. But why should he note the colour of the butterfly, the bright light of the sun, the hue of the wheat? This loveliness gave him no cheese for breakfast; of beauty in itself, for itself, he had no idea. How should he? To many of us the harvest—the summer—is a time of joy in light and colour; to him it was a time for adding yet another crust of hardness to the thick skin of his hands.

Though the haze looked like a mist it was perfectly dry; the wheat was as dry as noon; but a speck of dew, and the pimpernels wide open for a burning day. The reaping-machine began to rattle as he came up, and work was ready for him. At breakfast-time his fellows lent him a quarter of a loaf, some young onions, and a drink from their tea. He ate little, and the tea slipped from his hot tongue like water from the bars of a grate; his tongue was like the heated iron the housemaid tries before using it on the linen. As the reaping-machine went about the gradually decreasing square of corn, narrowing it by a broad band each time, the wheat fell flat on the short stubble. Roger stooped, and, gathering sufficient together, took a few straws, knotted them to another handful as you might tie two pieces of string, and twisted the band round the sheaf. He worked stooping to gather the wheat, bending to tie it in sheaves; stooping, bending—stooping, bending—and so across the field. Upon his head and back the fiery sun poured down the ceaseless and increasing heat of the August day. His face grew red, his neck black; the drought of the dry ground rose up and entered his mouth and nostrils; a warm air seemed to rise from the earth and fill his chest. His body ached from the ferment of the vile beer, his back ached with stooping, his forehead was bound tight with a brazen band. They brought some beer at last; it was like the spring in the desert to him. The vicious liquor—"a hair of the dog that bit him"—sank down his throat, grateful and refreshing to his disordered palate as if he had drunk the very shadow of green boughs. Good ale would have seemed nauseous to him at that moment, his taste and stomach destroyed by so many gallons of this. He was 'pulled together', and worked easier; the slow hours went on, and it was luncheon. He could have borrowed more food, but he was content instead with a screw of tobacco for his pipe and his allowance of beer.

They sat in the corner of the field. There were no trees for shade; they had been cut down as injurious to corn, but there were a few maple bushes and thin ash sprays, which seemed better than the open. The bushes cast no shade at all, the sun being so nearly overhead, but they formed a kind of enclosure, an open-air home, for men seldom sit down if they can help it on the bare and level plain; they go to the bushes, to the corner, or even to some hollow. It is not really any advantage; it is habit; or shall we not rather say that it is nature? Brought back as it were in the open field to the primitive conditions of life, they resumed the same instincts that controlled man in the ages past. Ancient man sought the shelter of trees and banks, of caves and hollows, and so the labourers under somewhat the same conditions came to the corner where the bushes grew. There they left their coats and slung up their luncheon-bundles to the branches; there the children played and took charge of the infants; there the women had their hearth and hung their kettle over a fire of sticks.

II

In August the unclouded sun, when there is no wind, shines as fervently in the harvest-field as in Spain. It is doubtful if the Spanish people feel the heat so much as our reapers; they have their siesta; their habits have become attuned to the sun, and it is no special strain upon them. In India our troops are carefully looked after in the hot weather, and everything made as easy for them as possible; without care and special clothing and coverings for the head they could not long endure. The English simoon of heat drops suddenly on the heads of the harvesters and finds them entirely unprepared; they have not so much as a cooling drink ready; they face it, as it were, unarmed. The sun spares not; it is fire from morn till night. Afar in the town the sunblinds are up, there is a tent on the lawn in the shade, people drink claret-cup and use ice; ice has never been seen in the harvest-field. Indoors they say they are melting lying on a sofa in a darkened room, made dusky to keep out the heat. The fire falls straight from the sky on the heads of the harvesters—men, women, and children—and the white-hot light beats up again from the dry straw and the hard ground.

The tender flowers endure; the wide petal of the poppy, which withers between the fingers, lies afloat on the air as the lilies on water, afloat and open to the weight of the heat. The red pimpernel looks straight up at the sky from the early morning till its hour of closing in the afternoon. Pale blue speedwell does not fade; the pale blue stands the warmth equally with the scarlet. Far in the thick wheat the streaked convolvulus winds up the stalks, and is not smothered for want of air though wrapped and circled with corn. Beautiful though they are, they are bloodless, not sensitive; we have given them our feelings, they do not share our pain or pleasure. Heat has gone into the hollow stalks of the wheat and down the yellow tubes to the roots, drying them in the earth. Heat has dried the leaves upon the hedge, and they touch rough—dusty rough, as books touch that have been lying unused; the plants on the bank are drying up and turning white. Heat has gone down into the cracks of the ground; the bar of the stile is so dry and powdery in the crevices that if a reaper chanced to drop a match on it there would seem risk of fire. The still atmosphere is laden with heat, and does not move in the corner of the field between the bushes.

Roger the reaper smoked out his tobacco; the children played round and watched for scraps of food; the women complained of the heat; the men said nothing. It is seldom that a labourer grumbles much at the weather, except as interfering with his work. Let the heat increase, so it would only keep fine. The fire in the sky meant money. Work went on again; Roger had now to go to another field to pitch—that is, help to load the waggon; as a young man, that was one of the jobs allotted to him. This was the reverse. Instead of stooping he had now to strain himself upright and lift sheaves over his head. His stomach empty of everything but small ale did not like this any more than his back had liked the other; but those who work for bare food must not question their employment. Heavily the day drove on; there was more beer, and again more beer, because it was desired to clear some fields that evening. Monotonously pitching the sheaves, Roger laboured by the waggon till the last had been loaded—till the moon was shining. His brazen forehead was unbound now; in spite of the beer the work and the perspiration had driven off the aching. He was weary but well. Nor had he been dull during the day; he had talked and joked—cumbrously in labourers' fashion—with his fellows. His aches, his empty stomach, his labour, and the heat had not overcome the vitality of his spirits. There was life enough left for a little rough play as the group gathered together and passed out through the gateway. Life enough left in him to go with the rest to the alehouse; and what else, oh moralist, would you have done in his place? This, remember, is not a fancy sketch of rural poetry; this is the reaper's real existence.

He had been in the harvest-field fourteen hours, exposed to the intense heat, not even shielded by a pith helmet; he had worked the day through with thew and sinew; he had had for food a little dry bread and a few onions, for drink a little weak tea and a great deal of small beer. The moon was now shining in the sky, still bright with sunset colours. Fourteen hours of sun and labour and hard fare! Now tell him what to do. To go straight to his plank-bed in the cowhouse; to eat a little more dry bread, borrow some cheese or greasy bacon, munch it alone, and sit musing till sleep came—he who had nothing to muse about. I think it would need a very clever man indeed to invent something for him to do, some way for him to spend his evening. Read! To recommend a man to read after fourteen hours burning sun is indeed a mockery; darn his stockings would be better. There really is nothing whatsoever that the cleverest and most benevolent person could suggest. Before any benevolent or well-meaning suggestions could be effective the preceding circumstances must be changed—the hours and conditions of labour, everything; and can that be done? The world has been working these thousands of years, and still it is the same; with our engines, our electric light, our printing press, still the coarse labour of the mine, the quarry, the field has to be carried out by human hands. While that is so, it is useless to recommend the weary reaper to read. For a man is not a horse: the horse's day's work is over; taken to his stable he is content, his mind goes no deeper than the bottom of his manger, and so long as his nose does not feel the wood, so long as it is met by corn and hay, he will endure happily. But Roger the reaper is not a horse.

Just as his body needed food and drink, so did his mind require recreation, and that chiefly consists of conversation. The drinking and the smoking are in truth but the attributes of the labourer's public-house evening. It is conversation that draws him thither, just as it draws men with money in their pockets to the club and the houses of their friends. Anyone can drink or smoke alone; it needs several for conversation, for company. You pass a public-house—the reaper's house—in the summer evening. You see a number of men grouped about trestle-tables out of doors, and others sitting at the open window; there is an odour of tobacco, a chink of glasses and mugs. You can smell the tobacco and see the ale; you cannot see the indefinite power which holds men there— the magnetism of company and conversation. *Their* conversation, not *your* conversation; not the last book, the last play; not saloon conversation; but theirs—talk in which neither you nor anyone of your condition could really join. To us there would seem nothing at all in that conversation, vapid and sub-jectless; to them it means much. We have not been through the same circum-stances: our day has been differently spent, and the same words have therefore a varying value. Certain it is, that it is conversation that takes men to the pub-lic-house. Had Roger been a horse, he would have hastened to borrow some food, and, having eaten that, would have cast himself at once upon his rude bed. Not being an animal, though his life and work were animal, he went with his friends to talk. Let none unjustly condemn him as a blackguard for that— no, not even though they had seen him at ten o'clock unsteadily walking to his shed, and guiding himself occasionally with his hands to save himself from stumbling. He blundered against the door, and the noise set the swallows on the beams twittering. He reached his bedstead, and sat down and tried to unlace his boots, but could not. He threw himself upon the sacks and fell asleep. Such was one twenty-four hours of harvest-time.

The next and the next, for weeks, were almost exactly similar; now a little less beer, now a little more; now tying up, now pitching, now cutting a small field or corner with a fagging-hook. Once now and then there was a great sup-per at the farm. Once he fell out with another fellow, and they had a fight; Roger, however, had had so much ale, and his opponent so much whisky, that

their blows were soft and helpless. They both fell—that is, they stumbled,—
they were picked up, there was some more beer, and it was settled. One afternoon Roger became suddenly giddy, and was so ill that he did no more work
that day, and very little on the following. It was something like a sunstroke,
but fortunately a slight attack; on the third day he resumed his place.
Continued labour in the sun, little food and much drink, stomach derange-
ment, in short, accounted for his illness. Though he resumed his place and
worked on, he was not so well afterwards; the work was more of an effort to
him, and his face lost its fulness, and became drawn and pointed. Still he
laboured, and would not miss an hour, for harvest was coming to an end, and
the extra wages would soon cease. For the first week or so of haymaking or
reaping the men usually get drunk, delighted with the prospect before them,
then they settle down fairly well. Towards the end they struggle hard to
recover lost time and the money spent in ale.

As the last week approached, Roger went up into the village and ordered
the shoemaker to make him a good pair of boots. He paid partly for them
then, and the rest next pay-day. This was a tremendous effort. The labourer
usually pays a shilling at a time, but Roger mistrusted himself. Harvest was
practically over, and after all the labour and the long hours, the exposure to the
sun and the rude lodging, he found he should scarcely have thirty shillings.
With the utmost ordinary care he could have saved a good lump of money. He
was a single man, and his actual keep cost but little. Many married labourers,
who had been forced by hard necessity to economy, contrived to put by
enough to buy clothes for their families. The single man, with every advantage,
hardly had thirty shillings, and even then it showed extraordinary prudence on
his part to go and purchase a pair of boots for the winter. Very few in his place
would have been as thoughtful as that; they would have got boots somehow in
the end, but not beforehand. This life of animal labour does not grow the spirit
of economy. Not only in farming, but in navvy work, in the rougher work of
factories and mines, the same fact is evident. The man who labours with thew
and sinew at horse labour—crane labour—not for himself, but for others, is
not the man who saves. If he worked for his own hand possibly he might, no
matter how rough his labour and fare; not while working for another. Roger
reached his distant home among the meadows at last, with one golden
half-sovereign in his pocket. That and his new pair of boots, not yet finished,
represented the golden harvest to him. He lodged with his parents when at
home; he was so far fortunate that he had a bed to go to; therefore in the esti-
mation of his class he was not badly off. But if we consider his position as
regards his own life we must recognize that he was very badly off indeed, so
much precious time and the strength of his youth having been wasted.

Often it is stated that the harvest wages recoup the labourer for the low weekly receipts of the year, and if the money be put down in figures with pen and ink it is so. But in actual fact the pen-and-ink figures do not represent the true case; these extra figures have been paid for, and gold may be bought too dear. Roger had paid heavily for his half-sovereign and his boots; his pinched face did not look as if he had benefited greatly. His cautious old father, rendered frugal by forty years of labour, had done fairly well; the young man not at all. The old man, having a cottage, in a measure worked for his own hand. The young man, with none but himself to think of, scattered his money to the winds. Is money earned with such expenditure of force worth the having? Look at the arm of a woman labouring in the harvest-field—thin, muscular, sinewy, black almost, it tells of continual strain. After much of this she becomes pulled out of shape, the neck loses its roundness and shows the sinews, the chest flattens. In time the women find the strain of it tell severely. I am not trying to make out a case of special hardship, being aware that both men, women, and children work as hard and perhaps suffer more in cities; I am simply describing the realities of rural life behind the scenes. The golden harvest is the first scene; the golden wheat, glorious under the summer sun. Bright poppies flower in its depths, and convolvulus climbs the stalks. Butterflies float slowly over the yellow surface as they might over a lake of colour. To linger by it, to visit it day by day, at even to watch the sunset by it, and see it pale under the changing light, is a delight to the thoughtful mind. There is so much in the wheat, there are books of meditation in it, it is dear to the heart. Behind these beautiful aspects comes the reality of human labour—hours upon hours of heat and strain; there comes the reality of a rude life, and in the end little enough of gain. The wheat is beautiful, but human life is labour.

Walks in the Wheat-fields

IF YOU WILL LOOK at a grain of wheat you will see that it seems folded up: it has crossed its arms and rolled itself up in a cloak, a fold of which forms a groove, and so gone to sleep. If you look at it sometime, as people in the old enchanted days used to look into a mirror, or the magic ink, until they saw living figures therein, you can almost trace a miniature human being in the oval of the grain. It is narrow at the top, where the head would be, and broad across the shoulders, and narrow again down towards the feet; a tiny man or woman has wrapped itself round about with a garment and settled to slumber. Up in the far north, where the dead ice reigns, our arctic explorers used to roll themselves in a sleeping-bag like this, to keep the warmth in their bodies against the chilliness of the night. Down in the south, where the heated sands of Egypt never cool, there in the rock-hewn tombs lie the mummies wrapped and lapped and wound about with a hundred yards of linen, in the hope, it may be, that spices and balm might retain within the sarcophagus some small fragment of human organism through endless ages, till at last the gift of life revisited it. Like a grain of wheat the mummy is folded in its cloth. And I do not know really whether I might not say that these little grains of English corn do not hold within them the actual flesh and blood of man. Transubstantiation is a fact there.

Sometimes the grains are dry and shrivelled and hard as shot, sometimes they are large and full and have a juiciness about them, sometimes they are a little bit red, others are golden, many white. The sack stands open in the market—you can thrust your arm in it a foot deep, or take up a handful and let it run back like a liquid stream, or hold it in your palm and balance it, feeling the weight. They are not very heavy as they lie in the palm, yet these little grains are a ponderous weight that rules man's world. Wherever they are there is empire. Could imperial Rome have only grown sufficient wheat in Italy to have fed her legions Caesar would still be master of three-fourths of the earth. Rome thought more in her latter days of grapes and oysters and mullets, that change colour as they die, and singing girls and flute-playing, and cynic verse of Horace—anything rather than corn. Rome is no more, and the lords of the world are they who have mastership of wheat. We have the mastership at this hour by dint of our gold and our hundred-ton guns, but they are telling our farmers to cast aside their corn, and to grow tobacco and fruit and anything else that can be thought of in preference. The gold is slipping away. These sacks in the market open to all to thrust their hands in are not sacks of corn but of golden sovereigns, half-sovereigns, new George and the dragon, old George and the dragon, Sydney mint sovereigns, Napoleons, half Napoleons, Belgian gold, German gold, Italian gold; gold scraped and scratched and gathered together like old rags from door to door. Sacks full of gold, verily I may say that all the gold poured out from the Australian fields, every pennyweight of it, hundreds of tons, all shipped over the sea to India, Australia, South Africa, Egypt, and, above all, America, to buy wheat. It was said that Pompey and his sons covered the great earth with their bones, for each one died in a different quarter of the world; but now he would want two more sons for Australia and America, the two new quarters which are now at work ploughing, sowing, reaping, without a month's intermission, growing corn for us. When you buy a bag of flour at the baker's you pay fivepence over the counter, a very simple transaction. Still you do not expect to get even that little bag of flour for nothing, your fivepence goes over the counter in somebody else's till. Consider now the broad ocean as the counter and yourself to represent thirty-five millions of English people buying sixteen, seventeen, or eighteen million quarters of wheat from the nations opposite, and paying for it shiploads of gold.

So that these sacks of corn in the market are truly filled with gold dust; and how strange it seems at first that our farmers, who are for ever dabbling with their hands in these golden sands, should be for ever grumbling at their poverty! 'The nearer the church the farther from God' is an old country proverb; the nearer to wheat the farther from mammon, I may construct as an addendum. Quite lately a gentleman told me that while he grew wheat on his thousand acres he lost just a pound an acre per annum, i.e. a thousand a year out of capital, so that if he had not happily given up this amusement he would now have been in the workhouse munching the putty there supplied for bread.

The rag and bone men go from door to door filling an old bag with scraps of linen, and so innumerable agents of bankers and financiers, vampires that suck gold, are for ever prowling about collecting every golden coin they can scent out and shipping it over sea. And what does not go abroad is in consequence of this great drain sharply locked up in the London safes as reserves against paper, and cannot be utilised in enterprises or manufacture. Therefore trade stands still, and factories are closed, and ship-yards are idle, and beautiful vessels are stored up doing nothing by hundreds in dock; coal mines left to be filled with water, and furnaces blown out. Therefore there is bitter distress and starvation, and cries for relief works, and one meal a day for Board school children, and the red flag of Socialism is unfurled. All because of these little grains of wheat.

They talked of bringing artillery, with fevered lips, to roar forth shrapnel in Trafalgar Square; why not Gatling guns? The artillery did not come for very shame, but the Guards did, and there were regiments of infantry in the rear, with glittering bayonets to prod folk into moving on. All about these little grains of wheat.

These thoughts came into my mind in the winter afternoon at the edge of a level cornfield, with the copper-sheathed spire of the village church on my right, the sun going down on the left. The copper did not gleam, it was dull and brown, no better than discoloured wood, patched with pieces of later date and another shade of dulness. I wish they would glitter, some of these steeples or some of our roofs, and so light up the reddish brown of the elms and the grey lichened oaks. The very rooks are black, and the starlings and the wintry fieldfares and redwings have no colour at a distance. They say the metal roofs and domes gleam in Russia, and even in France, and why not in our rare sunshine? Once now and then you see a gilded weathercock shine like a day-star as the sun goes down three miles away, over the dark brown field, where the plough has been going to and fro through the slow hours. I can see the plough and the horses very well at three miles, and know what they are doing.

I wish the trees, the elms, would grow tall enough and thick enough to hide the steeples and towers which stand up so stiff and stark, and bare and cold, some of them blunted and squab, some of them sharp enough to impale, with no more shape than a walking-stick, ferrule-upwards—every one of them out of proportion and jarring to the eye. If by good fortune you can find a spot where you cannot see a steeple or a church tower, where you can see only fields and woods, you will find it so much more beautiful, for nature has made it of its kind perfect. The dim sea is always so beautiful a view because it is not disfigured by these buildings. In the ships men live; in the houses among the trees they live; these steeples and towers are empty, and no spirit can dwell in that which is out of proportion. Scarcely any one can paint a picture of the country without sticking in one of these repellent structures. The oasthouses, whose red cones are so plentiful in Kent and Sussex, have quite a different effect; they have some colour, and by a curious felicity the builders have hit upon a good proportion, so that the shape is pleasant; these, too, have some use in the world.

Westward the sun was going down over the sea, and a wild west wind, which the glow of the sun as it touched the waves seemed to heat into fury, brought up the distant sound of the billows from the beach. A line of dark Spanish oaks from which the sharp pointed acorns were dropping, darkest green oaks, shut out the shore. A thousand starlings were flung up into the air out of these oaks, as if an impatient hand had cast them into the sky; then down they fell again, with a ceaseless whistling and clucking; up they went and down they came, lost in the deep green foliage as if they had dropped in the sea. The long level of the wheat-field plain stretched out from my feet towards the far-away Downs, so level that the first hedge shut off the fields beyond; and every now and then over these hedges there rose up the white forms of sea-gulls drifting to and fro among the elms. White sea-gulls—birds of divination, you might say—a good symbol of the times, for now we plough the ocean. The barren sea! In the Greek poets you may find constant reference to it as that which could not be reaped or sowed. Ulysses, to betoken his madness, took his plough down to the shore and drew furrows in the sand—the sea that even Demeter, great goddess, could not sow nor bring to any fruition. Yet now the ocean is our wheat-field and ships are our barns. The sea-gull should be painted on the village tavern sign instead of the golden wheatsheaf.

There could be no more flat and uninteresting surface than this field, a damp wet brown, water slowly draining out of the furrows, not a bird that I can see. No hare certainly, or partridge, or even a rabbit—nothing to sit or crouch—on that cold surface, tame and level as the brown cover of a book. They like something more human and comfortable; just as we creep into nooks and corners of rooms and into cosy arm-chairs, so they like tufts or some growth of shelter, or mounds that are dry, between hedges where there is a bite for them. I can trace nothing on this surface, so heavily washed by late rain. Let now the harriers come, and instantly the hounds' second sense of smell picks up the invisible sign of the hare that has crossed it in the night or early dawn, and runs it as swiftly as if he were lifting a clue of thread. The dull surface is all written over with hieroglyphics to the hound, he can read and translate to us in joyous tongue. Or the foxhounds carry a bee-line straight from hedge to hedge, and after them come the hoofs, prospecting deeply into the earth, dashing down fibre and blade, crunching up the tender wheat and battering it to pieces. It will rise again all the fresher and stronger, for there is something human in wheat, and the more it is trampled on the better it grows. Despots grind half the human race, and despots stronger than man—plague, pestilence, and famine—grind the whole; and yet the world increases, and the green wheat of the human heart is not to be trampled out.

The starlings grew busier and busier in the dark green Spanish oaks, thrown up as if a shell had burst among them; suddenly their clucking and whistling ceased, the speeches of contention were over, a vote of confidence had been passed in their Government, and the House was silent. The pheasants in the park shook their wings and crowed 'kuck, kuck—kow', and went to roost; the water in the furrows ceased to reflect; the dark earth grew darker and damper; the elms lost their reddish brown; the sky became leaden behind the ridge of the Downs, and the shadow of night fell over the field.

Twenty-five years ago I went into a camera obscura, where you see miniature men and women, coloured photographs alive and moving, trees waving, now and then dogs crossing the bright sun picture. I was only there a few moments, and I have never been in one since, and yet so inexplicable a thing is memory, the picture stands before me now clear as if it were painted and tangible. So many millions of pictures have come and gone upon the retina, and yet I can single out this one in an instant, and take it down as you would a book from a shelf. The millions of coloured etchings that have fixed themselves there in the course of those years are all in due order in the portfolio of the mind, and yet they cannot occupy the space of a pin's point. They have neither length, breadth, nor thickness, none of the qualifications of mathematical substance, and yet they must in some way be a species of matter. The fact indicates the possibility of still more subtle existences. Now I wish I could put before you a coloured, living, moving picture, like that of the camera obscura, of some other wheat-fields at a sunnier time. They were painted on the surface of a plain, set round about with a margin of green downs. They were large enough to have the charm of vague, indefinite extension, and yet all could be distinctly seen. Large squares of green corn that was absorbing its yellow from the sunlight, chess squares, irregularly placed, of brown furrows; others of rich blood-red trifolium; others of scarlet sainfoin and blue lucerne, gardens of scarlet poppies here and there. Not all of these, of course, at once, but they followed so quickly in the summer days that they seemed to be one and the same picture, and had you painted them altogether on the same canvas, together with ripe wheat, they would not have seemed out of place. Never was such brilliant colour; it was chalk there, and on chalk the colours are always clearer, the poppies deeper, the yellow mustard and charlock a keener yellow; the air, too, is pellucid. Waggons going along the tracks; men and women hoeing; ricks of last year still among clumps of trees, where the chimneys and gables of farmhouses are partly visible; red-tiled barns away yonder; a shepherd moving his hurdles; away again the black funnel of an idle engine, and the flywheel above hawthorn bushes—all so distinct and close under that you might almost fear to breathe for fear of dimming the mirror. The few white clouds sailing over seemed to belong to the fields on which their shadows were now foreshortened, now lengthened, as if they were really part of the fields, like the crops, and the azure sky so low down as to be the roof of the house and not at all a separate thing. And the sun a lamp that you might almost have pushed along his course faster with your hand; a loving and interesting sun that wanted the wheat to ripen, and stayed there in the slow-drawn arc of the summer day to lend a hand. Sun and sky and clouds close here and not across any planetary space, but working with us in the same field, shoulder to shoulder, with man. Then you might see the white doves yonder flutter up suddenly out of the trees by the farm, little flecks of white clouds themselves, and everywhere all throughout the plain an exquisite silence, a delicious repose, not one clang or harshness of sound to shatter the beauty of it. There you might stand on the high down among the thyme and watch it, hour after hour, and still no interruption; nothing to break it up. It was something like the broad folio of an ancient illuminated manuscript, in gold, gules, blue, green; with foliated scrolls and human figures, somewhat clumsy and thick, but quaintly drawn, and bold in their intense realism.

There was another wheat-field by the side of which I used to walk sometimes in the evenings, as the grains in the ears began to grow firm. The path ran for a mile beside it—a mile of wheat in one piece—all those million million stalks the same height, all with about the same number of grains in each ear, all ripening together. The hue of the surface travelled along as you approached; the tint of yellow shifted farther like the reflection of sunlight on water, but the surface was really much the same colour everywhere. It seemed a triumph of culture over such a space, such regularity, such perfection of myriads of plants springing in their true lines at the same time, each particular ear perfect, and a mile of it. Perfect work with the plough, the drill, the harrow in every detail, and yet such breadth. Let your hand touch the ears lightly as you walk—drawn through them as if over the side of a boat in water—feeling the golden heads. The sparrows fly out every now and then ahead; some of the birds like their corn as it hardens, and some while it is soft and full of milky sap. There are hares within, and many a brood of partridge chicks that cannot yet use their wings. Thick as the seed itself the feathered creatures have been among the wheat since it was sown. Finches more numerous than the berries on the hedges; sparrows like the finches multiplied by finches, linnets, rooks, like leaves on the trees, wood-pigeons whose crops are like bushel baskets for capacity; and now as it ripens the multitude will be multiplied by legions, and as it comes to the harvest there is a fresh crop of sparrows from the nests in the barns, you may see a brown cloud of them a hundred yards long. Besides which there were the rabbits that ate the young green blades, and the mice that will be busy in the sheaves, and the insects from spring-time to granary, a nameless host uncounted. A whole world, as it were, let loose upon the wheat, to eat, consume, and wither it, and yet it conquers the whole world. The great field you see was filled with gold corn four feet deep as a pitcher is filled with water to the brim. Of yore the rich man is

said, in the Roman classic, to have measured his money, so here you might
have measured it by the rood. The sunbeams sank deeper and deeper into the
wheat ears, layer upon layer of light, and the colour deepened by these daily
strokes. There was no bulletin to tell the folk of its progress, no Nileometer
to mark the rising flood of the wheat to its hour of overflow. Yet there went
through the village a sense of expectation, and men said to each other, "We
shall be there soon." No one knew the day—the last day of doom of the
golden race; everyone knew it was nigh. One evening there was a small square
piece cut at one side, a little notch, and two shocks stood there in the twilight.
Next day the village sent forth its army with their crooked weapons to cut and
slay. It used to be an era, let me tell you, when a great farmer gave the signal
to his reapers; not a man, woman, or child that did not talk of that.
Well-to-do people stopped their vehicles and walked out into the new stubble. Ladies came, farmers, men of low degree, everybody—all to exchange a
word or two with the workers. These were so terribly in earnest at the start
they could scarcely acknowledge the presence even of the squire. They felt
themselves so important, and were so full, and so intense and one-minded in
their labour, that the great of the earth might come and go as sparrows for
aught they cared. More men and more men were put on day by day, and
women to bind the sheaves, till the vast field held the village, yet they seemed
but a handful buried in the tunnels of the golden mine: they were lost in it
like the hares, for as the wheat fell, the shocks rose behind them, low tents of
corn. Your skin or mine could not have stood the scratching of the straw,
which is stiff and sharp, and the burning of the sun, which blisters like
red-hot iron. No one could stand the harvest-field as a reaper except he had
been born and cradled in a cottage, and passed his childhood bareheaded in
July heats and January snows. I was always fond of being out of doors, yet I
used to wonder how these men and women could stand it, for the summer
day is long, and they were there hours before I was up. The edge of the
reap-hook had to be driven by force through the stout stalks like a sword,
blow after blow, minute after minute, hour after hour; the back stooping, and
the broad sun throwing his fiery rays from a full disc on the head and neck. I
think some of them used to put handkerchiefs doubled up in their hats as
pads, as in the East they wind the long roll of the turban about the head, and
perhaps they would have done better if they had adopted the custom of the
South and wound a long scarf about the middle of the body, for they were
very liable to be struck down with such internal complaints as come from
great heat. Their necks grew black, much like black oak in old houses. Their
open chests were always bare, and flat, and stark, and never rising with
rounded bust-like muscle as the Greek statues of athletes.

The breast-bone was burned black, and their arms, tough as ash, seemed cased in leather. They grew visibly thinner in the harvest-field, and shrunk together—all flesh disappearing, and nothing but sinew and muscle remaining. Never was such work. The wages were low in those days, and it is not long ago, either—I mean the all-year-round wages; the reaping was piecework at so much per acre—like solid gold to men and women who had lived on dry bones, as it were, through the winter. So they worked and slaved, and tore at the wheat as if they were seized with a frenzy; the heat, the aches, the illness, the sunstroke, always impending in the air—the stomach hungry again before the meal was over, it was nothing. No song, no laugh, no stay—on from morn till night, possessed with a maddened desire to labour, for the more they could cut the larger the sum they would receive; and what is man's heart and brain to money? So hard, you see, is the pressure of human life that these miserables would have prayed on their knees for permission to tear their arms from the socket, and to scorch and shrivel themselves to charred human brands in the furnace of the sun.

Does it not seem bitter that it should be so? Here was the wheat, the beauty of which I strive in vain to tell you, in the midst of the flowery summer, scourging them with the knot of necessity; that which should give life pulling the life out of them, rendering their existence below that of the cattle, so far as the pleasure of living goes. Without doubt many a low mound in the churchyard—once visible, now level—was the sooner raised over the nameless dead because of that terrible strain in the few weeks of the gold fever. This is human life, real human life—no rest, no calm enjoyment of the scene, no generous gift of food and wine lavishly offered by the gods—the hard fist of necessity for ever battering man to a shapeless and hopeless fall.

The whole village lived in the field; a corn-land village is always the most populous, and every rood of land thereabouts, in a sense, maintains its man. The reaping, and the binding up and stacking of the sheaves, and the carting and building of the ricks, and the gleaning, there was something to do for every one, from the 'olde, olde, very olde man', the Thomas Parr of the hamlet, down to the very youngest child whose little eye could see, and whose little hand could hold a stalk of wheat. The gleaners had a way of binding up the collected wheat stalks together so that a very large quantity was held tightly in a very small compass. The gleaner's sheaf looked like the knot of a girl's hair woven in and bound. It was a tradition of the wheat-field handed down from generation to generation, a thing you could not possibly do unless you had been shown the secret—like the knots the sailors tie, a kind of hand art. The wheat-stalks being thick at one end makes the sheaf heavier and more solid there, and so in any manner of fastening it or stacking it, it takes a rounded shape like a nine-pin; the round ricks are built thick in the middle and lessen gradually toward the top and toward the ground. The warm yellow of the straw is very pleasant to look at on a winter's day under a grey sky; so, too, the straw looks nice and warm and comfortable, thrown down thickly in the yards for the roan cattle.

After the village has gone back to its home still the work of the wheat is not over; there is the thatching with straw of last year, which is bleached and contrasts with the yellow of the fresh-gathered crop. Next the threshing; and meantime the ploughs are at work, and very soon there is talk of seed-time.

I used to look with wonder when I was a boy at the endless length of wall and the enormous roof of a great tithe barn. The walls of Spanish convents, with little or no window to break the vast monotony, somewhat resemble it: the convent is a building, but does not look like a home; it is too big, too general. So this barn, with its few windows, seemed too immense to belong to any one man. The tithe barn has so completely dropped out of modern life that it may be well to briefly mention that its use was to hold the tenth sheaf from every wheat-field in the parish. The parson's tithe was the real actual tenth sheaf bodily taken from every field of corn in the district. A visible tenth, you see; a very solid thing. Imagine the vast heap they would have made, imagine the hundreds and hundreds of sacks of wheat they filled when they were threshed. I have often thought that it would perhaps be a good thing if this contribution of the real tenth could be brought back again for another purpose. If such a barn could be filled now, and its produce applied to the help of the poor and aged and injured of the village, we might get rid of that blot on our civilization—the workhouse. Mr Besant, in his late capital story, 'The Children of Gideon', most truly pointed out that it was custom which rendered all men indifferent to the sufferings of their fellow-creatures. In the old Roman days men were crucified so often that it ceased even to be a show; the soldiers played at dice under the miserable wretches; the peasant women stepping by jested and laughed and sang. Almost in our own time dry skeletons creaked on gibbets at every cross-road:

When for thirty shillings men were hung,
    And the thirst for blood grew stronger,
Men's lives were valued then at a sheep's—
    Thank God that lasts no longer.

So strong is custom and tradition, and the habit of thought it weaves about us, that I have heard ancient and grave farmers, when the fact was mentioned with horror, hum and ah! and handle their beards, and mutter that

they 'didn't know as 'twas altogether such a bad thing as they was hung for sheep-stealing.' There were parsons then, as now, in every rural parish preaching and teaching something they called the Gospel. Why did they not rise as one man and denounce this ghastly iniquity, and demand its abolition? They did nothing of the sort; they enjoyed their pipes and grog very comfortably.

The gallows at the cross-roads is gone, but the workhouse stands, and custom, cruel custom, that tyrant of the mind, has inured us (to use an old word) to its existence in our midst. Apart from any physical suffering, let us only consider the slow agony of the poor old reaper when he feels his lusty arm wither, and of the grey bowed wife as they feel themselves drifting like a ship ashore to that stony waiting-room. For it is a waiting-room till the grave receives them. Economically, too, the workhouse is a heavy loss and drag.

Could we, then, see the tithe barn filled again with golden wheat for this purpose of help to humanity, it might be a great and wonderful good. With this tenth to feed the starving and clothe the naked; with the tenth to give the little children a midday meal at the school—that would be natural and true. In the course of time, as the land laws lessen their grip, and the people take possession of the earth on which they stand, it is more than probable that something of this kind will really come about. It would be only simple justice after so many centuries—it takes so many hundreds of years to get even that.

'Workhouse, indeed!' I have heard the same ancient well-to-do greybeards ejaculate, 'workhouse! they ought to be very thankful they have got such a place to go to!'

All the village has been to the wheat-field with reaping-hooks, and waggons and horses, the whole strength of man has been employed upon it; little brown hands and large brown hands, blue eyes and dark eyes have been there searching about; all the intelligence of human beings has been brought to bear, and yet the stubble is not empty. Down there come again the ever-increasing clouds of sparrows; as a cloud rises here another cloud descends beyond it, a very mist and vapour as it were of wings. It makes one wonder to think where all the nests could have been; there could hardly have been enough eaves and barns for all these to have been bred in. Every one of the multitude has a keen pair of eyes and a hungry beak, and every single individual finds something to eat in the stubble. Something that was not provided for them, crumbs that have escaped from this broad table, and there they are every day for weeks together, still finding food. If you will consider the incredible number of little mouths, and the busy rate at which they ply them hour by hour, you may imagine what an immense number of grains of wheat must have escaped man's hand, for you must remember that every time they peck they take a whole grain. Down, too, come the grey-blue wood-pigeons and the wild turtle-doves. The singing linnets come in parties, the happy green-finches, the streaked yellowhammers, as if any one had delicately painted them in separate streaks, and not with a wash of colour, the brown buntings, chaffinches—out they come from the hazel copses, where the nuts are dropping, and the hedge berries turning red, and every one finds something to his liking. There are the seeds of the charlock and the thistle, and a hundred other little seeds, insects, and minute atom-like foods it needs a bird's eye to know. They are never still, they sweep up into the hedges and line the boughs, calling and talking, and away again to another rood of stubble without any order or plan of search, just sowing themselves about like wind-blown seeds. Up and down the day through with a zest never failing. It is beautiful to listen to them and watch them, if any one will stay under an oak by the nut-tree boughs, where the dragon-flies shoot to and fro in the shade as if the direct rays of the sun would burn their delicate wings; they hunt chiefly in the shade. The linnets will suddenly sweep up into the boughs and converse sweetly over your head. The sunshine lingers and grows sweeter as the autumn gives tokens of its coming in the buff bryony leaf, and the acorn filling its cup. They are so happy, the birds, yet there are few to listen to them. I have often looked round and wondered that no one else was about hearkening to them. Altogether, perhaps, they lead safer lives in England than anywhere else. We do not shoot them; the fowlers do mischief, still they make but little impression; there are few birds of prey, and there is not that fearful bloodthirstiness that makes a tropical forest so terrible in fact, under its outward show of glowing colour. There, with cruel hawks and owls, and serpents, and beasts of prey, a bird's life is one long terror. They are ever on the watch here, but they are not so fearfully harassed, and are not certain as it were beforehand to be torn to pieces. The land is well cultivated, and the more the culture the more the food for them. Frost and snow are their greatest enemies, but even these do not often last a great while. It is a land of woods, and above all of hedges, which are much more favourable to birds than forests, so that they are better off in England than in other countries. From the sowing to the reaping, the wheat-field gives a constant dole like the monasteries of old, only here it is no crust, but a free and bountiful largess. Then the stubble must be broken up by the plough, and again there is a fresh helping for them. Brown partridge, and black rook, and yellowhammer, all hues and degrees, come to the wheat-field.

Hours of Spring

IT IS SWEET on awaking in the early morn to listen to the small bird singing on the tree. No sound of voice or flute is like the bird's song; there is something in it distinct and separate from all other notes. The throat of woman gives forth a more perfect music, and the organ is the glory of man's soul. The bird upon the tree utters the meaning of the wind—a voice of the grass and wild flower, words of the green leaf; they speak through that slender tone. Sweetness of dew and rifts of sunshine, the dark hawthorn touched with breadths of open bud, the odour of the air, the colour of the daffodil— all that is delicious and beloved of spring-time are expressed in his song. Genius is nature, and his lay, like the sap in the bough from which he sings, rises without thought. Nor is it necessary that it should be a song; a few short notes in the sharp spring morning are sufficient to stir the heart. But yesterday the least of them all came to a bough by my window, and in his call I heard the sweet-briar wind rushing over the young grass. Refulgent fall the golden rays of the sun; a minute only, the clouds cover him and the hedge is dark. The bloom of the gorse is shut like a book; but it is there—a few hours of warmth and the covers will fall open. The meadow is bare, but in a little while the heart-shaped celandine leaves will come in their accustomed place. On the pollard willows the long wands are yellow-ruddy in the passing gleam of sunshine, the first colour of spring appears in their bark. The delicious wind rushes among them and they bow and rise; it touches the top of the dark pine that looks in the sun the same now as in summer; it lifts and swings the arching trail of bramble; it dries and crumbles the earth in its fingers; the hedge-sparrow's feathers are fluttered as he sings on the bush.

I wonder to myself how they can all get on without me—how they manage, bird and flower, without me to keep the calendar for them. For I noted it so carefully and lovingly, day by day, the seed-leaves on the mound in the sheltered places that come so early, the pushing up of the young grass, the succulent dandelion, the coltsfoot on the heavy, thick clods, the trodden chickweed despised at the foot of the gate-post, so common and small, and yet so dear to me. Every blade of grass was mine, as though I had planted it separately. They were all my pets, as the roses the lover of his garden tends so faithfully. All the grasses of the meadow were my pets, I loved them all; and perhaps that was why I never had a 'pet', never cultivated a flower, never kept a caged bird, or any creature. Why keep pets when every wild free hawk that passed overhead in the air was mine? I joyed in his swift, careless flight, in the throw of his pinions, in his rush over the elms and miles of woodland; it was happiness to see his unchecked life. What more beautiful than the sweep and curve of his going through the azure sky? These were my pets, and all the grass. Under the wind it seemed to dry and become grey, and the starlings running to and fro on the surface that did not sink now stood high above it and were larger. The dust that drifted along blessed it and it grew. Day by day a change; always a note to make. The moss drying on the tree trunks, dog's-mercury stirring under the ash-poles, bird's-claw buds of beech lengthening; books upon books to be filled with these things. I cannot think how they manage without me.

To-day through the window-pane I see a lark high up against the grey cloud, and hear his song. I cannot walk about and arrange with the buds and gorse-bloom; how does he know it is the time for him to sing? Without my book and pencil and observing eye, how does he understand that the hour has come? To sing high in the air, to chase his mate over the low stone wall of the ploughed field, to battle with his high-crested rival, to balance himself on his trembling wings outspread a few yards above the earth, and utter that sweet little loving kiss, as it were, of song—oh, happy, happy days! So beautiful to watch as if he were my own, and I felt it all! It is years since I went out amongst them in the old fields, and saw them in the green corn, they must be dead, dear little things, by now. Without me to tell him, how does this lark to-day that I hear through the window know it is his hour?

The green hawthorn buds prophesy on the hedge; the reed pushes up in the moist earth like a spear thrust through a shield; the eggs of the starling are laid in the knot-hole of the pollard elm—common eggs, but within each a speck that is not to be found in the cut diamond of two hundred carats—the dot of protoplasm, the atom of life. There was one row of pollards where they always began laying first. With a big stick in his beak the rook is blown aside like a loose feather in the wind; he knows his building-time from the fathers of his house—hereditary knowledge handed down in settled course: but the stray things of the hedge, how do they know? The great blackbird has planted his nest by the ash-stole, open to every one's view, without a bough to conceal it and not a leaf on the ash—nothing but the moss on the lower end of the branches. He does not seek cunningly for concealment. I think of the drift of time, and I see the apple bloom coming and the blue veronica in the grass. A thousand thousand buds and leaves and flowers and blades of grass, things to note day by day, increasing so rapidly that no pencil can put them down and no book hold them, not even to number them—and how to write the thoughts they give? All these without me—how can they manage without me?

For they were so much to me, I had come to feel that I was as much in return to them. The old, old error: I love the earth, therefore the earth loves me—I am her child—I am Man, the favoured of all creatures. I am the centre, and all for me was made.

In time past, strong of foot, I walked gaily up the noble hill that leads to Beachy Head from Eastbourne, joying greatly in the sun and the wind. Every step crumbled up numbers of minute grey shells, empty and dry, that crunched under foot like hoar-frost or fragile beads. They were very pretty; it

was a shame to crush them—such vases as no king's pottery could make. They lay by millions in the depths of the sward, and I thought as I broke them unwillingly that each of these had once been a house of life. A living creature dwelt in each and felt the joy of existence, and was to itself all in all—as if the great sun over the hill shone for it, and the width of the earth under was for it, and the grass and plants put on purpose for it. They were dead, the whole race of them, and these their skeletons were as dust under my feet. Nature sets no value upon life neither of minute hill-snail nor of human being.

I thought myself so much to the earliest leaf and the first meadow orchis—so important that I should note the first zee-zee of the titlark—that I should pronounce it summer, because now the oaks were green; I must not miss a day

nor an hour in the fields lest something should escape me. How beautiful the
droop of the great brome-grass by the wood! But to-day I have to listen to the
lark's song—not out of doors with him, but through the window-pane, and
the bullfinch carries the rootlet fibre to his nest without me. They manage
without me very well; they know their times and seasons—not only the civi-
lized rooks, with their libraries of knowledge in their old nests of reference, but
the stray things of the hedge and the chiffchaff from over sea in the ash wood.
They go on without me. Orchis flower and cowslip—I cannot number them
all—I hear, as it were, the patter of their feet—flower and bud and the beautiful clouds that go over, with the sweet rush of rain and burst of sun glory
among the leafy trees. They go on, and I am no more than the least of the
empty shells that strewed the sward of the hill. Nature sets no value upon life,
neither of mine nor of the larks that sang years ago. The earth is all in all to
me, but I am nothing to the earth: it is bitter to know this before you are dead.
These delicious violets are sweet for themselves; they were not shaped and
coloured and gifted with that exquisite proportion and adjustment of odour
and hue for me. High up against the grey cloud I hear the lark through the
window singing, and each note falls into my heart like a knife.

Now this to me speaks as the roll of thunder that cannot be denied—you
must hear it; and how can you shut your ears to what this lark sings, this violet tells, this little grey shell writes in the curl of its spire? The bitter truth that
human life is no more to the universe than that of the unnoticed hill-snail in
the grass should make us think more and more highly of ourselves as human—
as men—living things that think. We must look to ourselves to help ourselves.
We must think ourselves into an earthly immortality. By day and by night, by
years and by centuries, still striving, studying, searching to find that which
shall enable us to live a fuller life upon the earth—to have a wider grasp upon
its violets and loveliness, a deeper draught of the sweet-briar wind. Because my
heart beats feebly to-day, my trickling pulse scarcely notating the passing of the
time, so much the more do I hope that those to come in future years may see
wider and enjoy fuller than I have done; and so much the more gladly would
I do all that I could to enlarge the life that shall be then. There is no hope on
the old lines—they are dead, like the empty shells; from the sweet delicious
violets think out fresh petals of thought and colours, as it were, of soul.

Never was such a worshipper of earth. The commonest pebble, dusty and
marked with the stain of the ground, seems to me so wonderful; my mind
works round it till it becomes the sun and centre of a system of thought and
feeling. Sometimes moving aside the tufts of grass with careless fingers while
resting on the sward, I found these little pebble-stones loose in the crumbly
earth among the rootlets. Then, brought out from the shadow, the sunlight

shone and glistened on the particles of sand that adhered to it. Particles adhered to my skin—thousands of years between finger and thumb, these atoms of quartz, and sunlight shining all that time, and flowers blooming and life glowing in all, myriads of living things, from the cold still limpet on the rock to the burning, throbbing heart of man. Sometimes I found them among the sand of the heath, the sea of golden brown surging up yellow billows six feet high about me, where the dry lizard hid, or basked, of kin, too, to old time. Or the rush of the sea wave brought them to me, wet and gleaming, up from the depths of what unknown Past? where they nestled in the root crevices of trees forgotten before Egypt. The living mind opposite the dead pebble—did you ever consider the strange and wonderful problem there? Only the thickness of the skin of the hand between them. The chief use of matter is to demonstrate to us the existence of the soul. The pebble-stone tells me I am a soul because I am not that that touches the nerves of my hand. We are distinctly two, utterly separate, and shall never come together. The little pebble and the great sun overhead—millions of miles away: yet is the great sun no more distinct and apart than this which I can touch. Dull-surfaced matter, like a polished mirror, reflects back thought to thought's self within.

I listened to the sweet-briar wind this morning; but for weeks and weeks the stark black oaks stood straight out of the snow as masts of ships with furled sails frozen and ice-bound in the haven of the deep valley. Each was visible to the foot, set in the white slope, made individual in the wood by the brilliance of the background. Never was such a long winter. For fully two months they stood in the snow in black armour of iron bark unshaken, the front rank of the forest army that would not yield to the northern invader. Snow in broad flakes, snow in semi-flakes, snow raining down in frozen specks, whirling and twisting in fury, ice raining in small shot of frost, howling, sleeting, groaning; the ground like iron, the sky black and faintly yellow—brutal colours of despotism—heaven striking with clenched fist. When at last the general surface cleared, still there remained the trenches and traverses of the enemy, his ramparts drifted high, and his roads marked with snow. The black firs on the ridge stood out against the frozen clouds, still and hard; the slopes of leafless larches seemed withered and brown; the distant plain far down gloomy with the same dull yellowish blackness. At a height of seven hundred feet the air was sharp as a scythe—a rude barbarian giant wind knocking at the walls of the house with a vast club, so that we crept sideways even to the windows to look out upon the world. There was everything to repel—the cold, the frost, the hardness, the snow, dark sky and ground, leaflessness; the very furze chilled and all benumbed. Yet the forest was still beautiful. There was no day that we did not, all of us, glance out at it and admire it, and say something about it. Harder and harder grew the frost, yet still the forest-clad hills possessed a something that drew the mind open to their largeness and grandeur. Earth is always beautiful—always. Without colour, or leaf, or sunshine, or song of bird and flutter of butterfly's wing; without anything sensuous, without advantage or gilding of summer—the power is ever there. Or shall we not say that the desire of the mind is ever there, and *will* satisfy itself, in a measure at least, even with the barren wild? The heart from the moment of its first beat instinctively longs for the beautiful; the means we possess to gratify it are limited—we are always trying to find the statue in the rude block. Out of the vast block of the earth the mind endeavours to carve itself loveliness, nobility, and grandeur. We strive for the right and the true: it is circumstance that thrusts wrong upon us.

One morning a labouring man came to the door with a spade, and asked if he could dig the garden, or try to, at the risk of breaking the tool in the ground. He was starving; he had had no work for two months; it was just six months, he said, since the first frost started the winter. Nature and the earth and the gods did not trouble about *him*, you see; he might grub the rockfrost ground with his hands if he chose—the yellowish black sky did not care. Nothing for man! The only good he found was in his fellow-men; they fed him after a fashion— still they fed him. There was no good in anything else. Another aged man came once a week regularly; white as the snow through which he walked. In summer he worked; since the winter began he had had no employment, but supported himself by going round to the farms in rotation. They all gave him a trifle— bread and cheese, a penny, a slice of meat—something; and so he lived, and slept the whole of that time in outhouses wherever he could. He had no home of any kind. Why did he not go into the workhouse? 'I be afeared if I goes in there they'll put me with the rough uns, and very likely I should get some of my clothes stole.' Rather than go into the workhouse he would totter round in the face of the blasts that might cover his weak old limbs with drift. There was a sense of dignity and manhood left still; his clothes were worn, but clean and decent; he was no companion of rogues; the snow and frost, the straw of the outhouses, was better than that. He was struggling against age, against nature, against circumstance; the entire weight of society, law, and order pressed upon him to force him to lose his self-respect and liberty. He would rather risk his life in the snowdrift. Nature, earth, and the gods did not help him; sun and stars, where were they? He knocked at the doors of the farms and found good in man only—not in Law or Order, but in individual man alone.

The bitter north wind drives even the wild fieldfare to the berries in the garden hedge; so it drives stray human creatures to the door. A third came—an old gipsy woman—still stout and hearty, with green fresh brooms to sell. We bought some brooms—one of them was left on the kitchen floor, and the tame rabbit nibbled it; it proved to be heather. The true broom is as green and succulent in appearance in January as June. She would see the 'missis'. 'Bless you, my good lady, it be weather, bean't it? I hopes you'll never know what it be to want, my good lady. Ah, well, you looks good-tempered if you don't want to buy nothing. Do you see if you can't find me an old body, now, for my girl—now do 'ee try; she's confined in a tent on the common—nothing but one of our tents, my good lady—that's true—and she's doing jest about well,' (with briskness and an air of triumph) 'that she is! She's got twins, you see, my lady, but she's all right, and as well as can be. She wants to get up; and she says to me, 'Mother, do 'ee try and get me a body; 'tis hard to lie here abed and be well enough to get up, and be obliged to stay here because I've got nothing but a bedgown.' For you see, my good lady, we managed pretty well with the first baby; but the second bothered us, and we cut up all the bits of things we could find, and there she ain't got nothing to put on. Do 'ee see if 'ee can't find her an old body.' The common is an open piece of furze and heath at the verge of the forest; and here, in a tent just large enough to creep in, the gipsy woman had borne twins in the midst of the snow and frost. They could not make a fire of the heath and gorse even if they cut it, the snow and whirling winds would not permit. The old gipsy said if they had little food they could not do without fire, and they were compelled to get coke and coal somehow—apologizing for such a luxury. There was no whining—not a bit of it; they were evidently quite contented and happy, and the old woman proud of her daughter's hardihood. By-and-by the husband came round with straw beehives to sell, and cane to mend chairs—a strong, respectable-looking man. Of all the north wind drove to the door, the outcasts were the best off—much better off than the cottager who was willing to break his spade to earn a shilling; much better off than the white-haired labourer, whose strength was spent, and who had not even a friend to watch with him in the dark hours of the winter evening—not even a fire to rest by. The gipsy nearest to the earth was the best off in every way; yet not even for primitive man and woman did the winds cease. Broad flakes of snow drifted up against the low tent, beneath which the babes were nestling to the breast. Not even for the babes did the snow cease or the keen wind rest; the very fire could scarcely struggle against it. Snow-rain and ice-rain; frost-formed snow-granules, driven along like shot, stinging and rattling against the tent-cloth, hissing in the fire; roar and groan of the great wind among the oaks of the forest. No kindness to man, from birth-hour to ending; neither earth, sky, nor gods care for him, innocent at the mother's breast. Nothing good to man but man. Let man, then, leave his gods and lift up his ideal beyond them.

Something grey and spotted and puffy, not unlike a toad, moved about under the gorse of the garden hedge one morning, half hidden by the stalks of old grasses. By-and-by it hopped out—the last thrush, so distended with puffed feathers against the frost as to be almost shapeless. He searched about hopelessly round the stones and in the nooks, all hard and frostbound; there was the shell of a snail, dry and whitened and empty, as was apparent enough even at a distance. His keen eye must have told him that it was empty; yet such was his hunger and despair that he took it and dashed it to pieces against a stone. Like a human being, his imagination was stronger than his experience; he tried to persuade himself that there might be something there; hoping against hope. Mind, you see, working in the bird's brain, and overlooking facts. A mere mechanism would have left the empty and useless shell untouched— would have accepted facts at once, however bitter, just as the balance on the heaviest side declines immediately, obeying the fact of an extra grain of weight. The bird's brain was not mechanical, and therefore he was not wholly mastered by experience. It was a purely human action—just what we do ourselves. Next he came across to the door to see if a stray berry still remained on a creeper. He saw me at the window, and he came to the window—right to it—and stopped and looked full at me some minutes, within touch almost, saying as plainly as could be said, "I am starving—help me." I never before knew a thrush make so unmistakable an appeal for assistance, or deliberately approach so near (unless previously encouraged). We tried to feed him, but we fear little of the food reached him. The wonder of the incident was that a thrush should still be left—there had not been one in the garden for two months. Berries all gone, ground hard and foodless, streams frozen, snow lying for weeks, frost stealing away the vital heat—ingenuity could not devise a more terrible scene of torture to the birds. Neither for the thrushes nor for the new-born infants in the tent did the onslaught of the winter slacken. No pity in earth or heaven. This one thrush did, indeed, by some exceptional fortune, survive; but where were the family of thrushes that had sung so sweetly in the rainy autumn? Where were the blackbirds?

Looking down from the stilts of seven hundred feet into the deep coombe of black oaks standing in the white snow, day by day, built round about with the rugged mound of the hills, doubly locked with the key of frost—it seemed to me to take on itself the actuality of the ancient faith of the Magi. How the seeds of all living things—the germs—of bird and animal, man and insect, tree and herb, of the whole earth—were gathered together into a four-square rampart, and there laid to sleep in safety, shielded by a spell-bound fortification against the coming flood, not of water, but of frost and snow! With snow and frost and winter the earth was overcome, and the world perished, stricken dumb and dead, swept clean and utterly destroyed—a winter of the gods, the silence of snow and universal death. All that had been passed away, and the earth was depopulated. Death triumphed. But under the snow, behind the charmed rampart, slept the living germs. Down in the deep coombe, where the dark oaks stood out individually in the whiteness of the snow, fortified round about with immovable hills, there was the actual presentment of Zoroaster's sacred story. Locked in sleep lay bud and germ—the butterflies of next summer were there somewhere, under the snow. The earth was swept of its inhabitants, but the seeds of life were not dead. Near by were the tents of the gipsies—an Eastern race, whose forefathers perhaps had seen that very Magian worship of the Light; and in those tents birth had already taken place. Under the Night of winter—under the power of dark Ahriman, the evil spirit of Destruction—lay bud and germ in bondage, waiting for the coming of Ormuzd, the Sun of Light and Summer. Beneath the snow, and in the frozen crevices of the trees, in the chinks of the earth, sealed up by the signet of frost, were the seeds of the life that would replenish the air in time to come. The buzzing crowds of summer were still under the snow.

This forest land is marked by the myriads of insects that roam about it in the days of sunshine. Of all the million million heathbells—multiply them again by a million million more—that purple the acres of rolling hills, mile upon mile, there is not one that is not daily visited by these flying creatures. Countless and incalculable hosts of the yellow-barred hover-flies come to them; the heath and common, the moor and forest, the hedgerow and copse, are full of insects. They rise under foot, they rise from the spray brushed by your arm as you pass, they settle down in front of you—a rain of insects, a coloured shower. Legion is a little word for the butterflies; the dry pastures among the woods are brown with meadow-brown; blues and coppers float in endless succession; all the nations of Xerxes' army were but a handful to these. In their millions they have perished; but somewhere, coiled up, as it were, and sealed under the snow, there must have been the mothers and germs of the equally vast crowds that will fill the atmosphere this year. The great humble-bee that shall be mother of hundreds, the yellow wasp that shall be mother of thousands, were hidden there somewhere. The food of the migrant birds that are coming from over sea was there dormant under the snow. Many nations have a tradition of a former world destroyed by a deluge of water, from the East to the West, from Greece to Mexico, where the tail of a comet was said to have caused the flood; but in the strange characters of the Zend is the legend of an ark (as it were) prepared against the snow. It may be that it is the dim memory of a glacial epoch. In this deep coombe, amid the dark oaks and snow, was the fable of Zoroaster. For the coming of Ormuzd, the

Light and Life Bringer, the leaf slept folded, the butterfly was hidden, the germ concealed, while the sun swept upwards towards Aries.

There is nothing so wearying as a long frost—the endless monotony, which makes one think that the very fault we usually find with our climate—its changeableness—is in reality its best quality. Rain, mist, gales—anything; give us anything but weary, weary frost. But having once fixed its mind, the weather will not listen to the usual signs of alteration.

The larks sang at last high up against the grey cloud over the frost-bound earth. They could not wait longer; love was strong in their little hearts—stronger than the winter. After a while the hedge-sparrows, too, began to sing on the top of the gorse-hedge about the garden. By-and-by a chaffinch boldly raised his voice, ending with the old story, 'Sweet, will you, will you kiss—me—dear?' Then there came a hoar-frost, and the earth, which had been black, became white, as its evaporated vapours began to gather and drops of rain to fall. Even then the obstinate weather refused to quite yield, wrapping its cloak, as it were, around it in bitter enmity. But in a day or two white clouds lit up with sunshine appeared drifting over from the southward, and that was the end. The old pensioner came to the door for his bread and cheese: "The wind's in the south," he said, "and I hopes she'll stay there." Five dull yellow spots on the hedge—gorse bloom—that had remained unchanged for so many weeks, took a fresh colour and became golden. By the constant passing of the waggons and carts along the road that had been so silent it was evident that the busy time of spring was here. There would be rough weather, doubtless, now and again, but it would not again be winter.

Dark patches of cloud—spots of ink on the sky, the 'messengers'—go drifting by; and after them will follow the water-carriers, harnessed to the south and west winds, drilling the long rows of rain like seed into the earth. After a time there will be a rainbow. Through the bars of my prison I can see the catkins thick and sallow-grey on the willows across the field, visible even at that distance; so great the change in a few days, the hand of spring grows firm and takes a strong grasp of the hedges. My prison bars are but a sixteenth of an inch thick; I could snap them with a fillip—only the window-pane, to me as impenetrable as the twenty-foot wall of the Tower of London. A cart has just gone past bearing a strange load among the carts of spring; they are talking of poling the hops. In it there sat an old man, with the fixed stare, the animal-like eye, of extreme age; he is over ninety. About him there were some few chairs and articles of furniture, and he was propped against a bed. He was being moved—literally carted—to another house, not home, and he said he could not go without his bed; he had slept on it for seventy-three years. Last Sunday his son—himself old—was carted to the churchyard, as is the country custom, in an open van; to-day the father, still living, goes to what will be to him a strange land. His home is broken up—he will potter no more with maize for the chicken; the gorse hedges will become solid walls of golden bloom, but there will never again be a spring for him. It is very hard, is it not, at ninety? It is not the tyranny of any one that has done it; it is the tyranny of circumstance, the lot of man. The song of the Greeks is full of sorrow; man was to them the creature of grief, yet theirs was the land of violets and pellucid air. This has been a land of frost and snow, and here, too, it is the same. A stranger, I see, is already digging the old man's garden.

How happy the trees must be to hear the song of birds again in their branches! After the silence and the leaflessness, to have the birds back once more and to feel them busy at the nest-building; how glad to give them the moss and fibres and the crutch of the boughs to build in! Pleasant it is now to watch the sunlit clouds sailing onwards; it is like sitting by the sea. There is voyaging to and fro of birds; the strong wood-pigeon goes over—a long course in the air, from hill to distant copse; a blackbird starts from an ash, and, now inclining this way and now that, traverses the meadows to the thick corner hedge; finches go by, and the air is full of larks that sing without ceasing. The touch of the wind, the moisture of the dew, the sun-stained raindrop, have in them the magic force of life—a marvellous something that was not there before. Under it the narrow blade of grass comes up freshly green between the old white fibres the rook pulled; the sycamore bud swells and opens, and takes the eye instantly in the still dark wood; the starlings go to the hollow pollards; the lambs leap in the mead. You never know what a day may bring forth— what new thing will come next. Yesterday I saw the ploughman and his team, and the earth gleam smoothed behind the share; to-day a butterfly has gone past; the farm-folk are bringing home the fagots from the hedgerows; to-morrow there will be a merry, merry note in the ash copse, the chiffchaffs' ringing call to arms, to arms, ye leaves! By-and-by a bennet, a bloom of the grass; in time to come the furrow, as it were, shall open, and the great buttercup of the waters will show a broad palm of gold. You never know what will come to the net of the eye next—a bud, a flower, a nest, a curled fern, or whether it will be in the woodland or by the meadow path, at the water's side or on the dead dry heap of fagots. There is no settled succession, no fixed and formal order— always the unexpected; and you cannot say, 'I will go and find this or that.' The sowing of life in the spring time is not in the set straight line of the drill, nor shall you find wild flowers by a foot measure. There are great woods without a lily of the valley; the nightingale does not sing everywhere. Nature has no arrangement, no plan, nothing judicious even; the walnut trees bring forth their tender buds, and the frost burns them—they have no mosaic of time to fit in, like a Roman tesselated pavement; nature is like a child, who will sing and shout though you may be never so deeply pondering in the study, and does not wait for the hour that suits your mind. You do not know what you may find each day; perhaps you may only pick up a fallen feather, but it is beautiful, every filament. Always beautiful! everything beautiful! And are these things new—the ploughman and his team, the lark's song, the green leaf! Can they be new? Surely they have been of old time! They are, indeed, new—the only things that are so; the rest is old and grey, and a weariness.

Nature and Books

WHAT IS THE COLOUR of the dandelion? There are many dandelions: that which I mean flowers in May, when the meadow-grass has started and the hares are busy by daylight. That which flowers very early in the year has a thickness of hue, and is not interesting; in autumn the dandelions quite change their colour and are pale. The right dandelion for this question is the one that comes about May with a very broad disc, and in such quantities as often to cover a whole meadow. I used to admire them very much in the fields by Surbiton (strong clay soil), and also on the towing-path of the Thames where the sward is very broad, opposite Long Ditton; indeed, I have often walked up that towing-path on a beautiful sunny morning, when all was quiet except the nightingales in the Palace hedge, on purpose to admire them. I dare say they are all gone now for evermore; still, it is a pleasure to look back on anything beautiful. What colour is this dandelion? It is not yellow, nor orange, nor gold; put a sovereign on it and see the difference. They say the gipsies call it the Queen's great hairy dog-flower—a number of words to one stalk; and so, to get a colour to it, you may call it the yellow-gold-orange plant. In the winter, on the black mud under a dark, dripping tree, I found a piece of orange peel, lately dropped—a bright red orange speck in the middle of the blackness. It looked very beautiful, and instantly recalled to my mind the great dandelion discs in the sunshine of summer. Yet certainly they are not red-orange. Perhaps, if ten people answered this question, they would each give different answers. Again, a bright day or a cloudy, the presence of a slight haze, or the juxtaposition of other colours, alters it very much; for the dandelion is not a glazed colour, like the buttercup, but sensitive. It is like a sponge, and adds to its own hue that which is passing, sucking it up.

The shadows of the trees in the wood, why are they blue? Ought they not to be dark? Is it really blue, or an illusion? And what is their colour when you see the shadow of a tall trunk aslant in the air like a leaning pillar? The fallen brown leaves wet with dew have a different brown from those that are dry, and the upper surface of the green growing leaf is different from the under surface. The yellow butterfly, if you meet one in October, has so toned down his spring yellow that you might fancy him a pale green leaf floating along the road. There is a shining, quivering, gleaming; there is a changing, fluttering, shifting; there is a mixing, weaving—varnished wings, translucent wings, wings with dots and veins, all playing over the purple heath; a very tangle of many-toned lights and hues. Then come the apples: if you look upon them from an upper window, so as to glance along the level plane of the fruit, delicate streaks of scarlet, like those that lie parallel to the eastern horizon before sunrise; golden tints under bronze, and apple-green, and some that the wasps have hollowed, more glowingly beautiful than the rest; sober leaves and black and white swallows: to see it you must be high up, as if the apples were strewn on a sward of foliage. So have I gone in three steps from May dandelion to September apple; an immense space measured by things beautiful, so filled that ten folio volumes could not hold the description of them, and I have left out the meadows, the brooks, and hills. Often in writing about these things I have felt very earnestly my own incompetence to give the least idea of their brilliancy and many-sided colours. My gamut was so very limited in its terms, and would not give a note to one in a thousand of those I saw. At last I said, I will have more words; I will have more terms; I will have a book on colour, and I will find and use the right technical name for each one of these lovely tints. I was told that the very best book was by Chevreul, which had tinted illustrations, chromatic scales, and all that could be desired.

Quite true, all of it; but for me it contained nothing. There was a good deal about assorted wools, but nothing about leaves; nothing by which I could tell you the difference between the light scarlet of one poppy and the deep purple-scarlet of another species. The dandelion remained unexplained; as for the innumerable other flowers, and wings, and sky-colours, they were not even approached. The book, in short, dealt with the artificial and not with nature. Next I went to science—works on optics, such a mass of them. Some I had read in old time, and turned to again; some I read for the first time, some translated from the German, and so on. It appeared that, experimenting with physical colour, tangible paint, they had found out that red, yellow, and blue were the three primary colours; and then, experimenting with light itself, with colours not tangible, they found out that red, green, and violet were the three primary colours; but neither of these would do for the dandelion. Once upon a time I had taken an interest in spectrum analysis, and the theory of the polarisation of light was fairly familiar; any number of books, but not what I wanted to know. Next the idea occurred to me of buying all the colours used in painting, and tinting as many pieces of paper a separate hue, and so comparing these with petals, and wings, and grass, and trifolium. This did not answer at all; my unskilful hands made a very poor wash, and the yellow paper set by a yellow petal did not agree, the scientific reason of which I cannot enter into now. Secondly, the names attached to many of these paints are unfamiliar to general readers; it is doubtful if bistre, Leitch's blue, oxide of chromium, and so on, would convey an idea. They might as well be Greek symbols: no use to attempt to describe hues of heath or hill in that way. These, too, are only distinct colours. What was to be done with all the shades and tones? Still there remained the language of the studio; without doubt a master of painting could be found who would quickly supply the technical term of anything I liked to show him; but again no use, because it would be technical. And a still more unsurmountable difficulty occurs: in so

far as I have looked at pictures, it seems as if the artists had met with the same obstacle in paints as I have in words—that is to say, a deficiency. Either painting is incompetent to express the extreme beauty of nature, or in some way the canons of art forbid the attempt. Therefore I had to turn back, throw down my books with a bang, and get me to a bit of fallen timber in the open air to meditate.

Would it be possible to build up a fresh system of colour language by means of natural objects? Could we say pine-wood green, larch green, spruce green, wasp yellow, humble-bee amber? And there are fungi that have marked tints, but the Latin names of these agarics are not pleasant. Butterfly blue— but there are several varieties; and this plan is interfered with by two things: first, that almost every single item of nature, however minute, has got a distinctly different colour, so that the dictionary of tints would be immense; and next, so very few would know the object itself that the colour attached to it would have no meaning. The power of language has been gradually enlarging for a great length of time, and I venture to say that the English language at the present time can express more, and is more subtle, flexible, and, at the same time, vigorous, than any of which we possess a record. When people talk to me about studying Sanscrit, or Greek, or Latin, or German, or, still more absurd, French, I feel as if I could fell them with a mallet happily. Study the

English, and you will find everything there, I reply. With such a language I fully anticipate, in years to come, a great development in the power of expressing thoughts and feelings which are now thoughts and feelings only. How many have said of the sea, "It makes me feel something I cannot say!" Hence it is clear there exists in the intellect a layer, if I may so call it, of thought yet dumb-chambers within the mind which require the key of new words to unlock. Whenever that is done a fresh impetus is given to human progress. There are a million books, and yet with all their aid I cannot tell you the colour of the May dandelion. There are three greens at this moment in my mind: that of the leaf of the flower-de-luce, that of the yellow iris leaf, and that of the bayonet-like leaf of the common flag. With admission to a million books, how am I to tell you the difference between these tints? So many, many books, and such a very, very little bit of nature in them! Though we have been so many thousand years upon the earth we do not seem to have done any more as yet than walk along beaten footpaths, and sometimes really it would seem as if there were something in the minds of many men quite artificial, quite distinct from the sun and trees and hills—altogether house people, whose gods must be set in four-cornered buildings. There is nothing in books that touches my dandelion.

It grows, ah yes, it grows! How does it grow? Builds itself up somehow of sugar and starch, and turns mud into bright colour and dead earth into food for bees, and some day perhaps for you, and knows when to shut its petals, and how to construct the brown seeds to float with the wind, and how to please the children, and how to puzzle me. Ingenious dandelion! If you find out that its correct botanical name is *Leontodon taraxacum*, or *Leontodon dens-leonis*, that will bring it into botany; and there is a place called Dandelion Castle in Kent, and a bell with the inscription—

> John de Dandelion with his great dog
> Brought over this bell on a mill cog—

which is about as relevant as the mere words *Leontodon taraxacum*. Botany is the knowledge of plants according to the accepted definition; naturally, therefore, when I began to think I would like to know a little more of flowers than could be learned by seeing them in the fields, I went to botany. Nothing could be more simple. You buy a book which first of all tells you how to recognize them, how to classify them; next instructs you in their uses, medical or economical; next tells you about the folk-lore and curious associations; next enters into a lucid explanation of the physiology of the plant and its relation to other creatures; and finally, and most important, supplies you with the ethical feeling, the ideal aspiration to be identified with each particular flower.

One moderately thick volume would probably suffice for such a modest round as this.

Lo! now the labour of Hercules when he set about bringing up Cerberus from below, and all the work done by Apollo in the years when he ground corn, are but a little matter compared with the attempt to master botany. Great minds have been at it these two thousand years, and yet we are still only nibbling at the edge of the leaf, as the ploughboys bite the young hawthorn in spring. The mere classification—all plant-lore was a vast chaos till there came the man of Sweden, the great Linnaeus, till the sexes were recognized, and everything was ruled out and set in place again. A wonderful man! I think it would be true to say it was Linnaeus who set the world on its present twist of thinking, and levered our mental globe a little more perpendicular to the ecliptic. He actually gathered the dandelion and took it to bits like a scientific child; he touched nature with his fingers instead of sitting looking out of window—perhaps the first man who had ever done so for seventeen hundred years or so, since superstition blighted the progress of pagan Rome. The work he did! But no one reads Linnaeus now; the folios, indeed, might moulder to dust without loss, because his spirit has got into the minds of men, and the text is of little consequence. The best book he wrote to read now is the delightful *Tour in Lapland*, with its quaint pen-and-ink sketches, so realistically vivid, as if the thing sketched had been banged on the paper and so left its impress. I have read it three times, and I still cherish the old yellow pages; it is the best botanical book, written by the greatest of botanists, specially sent on a botanical expedition, and it contains nothing about botany. It tells you about the canoes, and the hard cheese, and the Laplander's warehouse on top of a pole, like a pigeon-house; and the innocent way in which the maiden helped the traveller in his bath, and how the aged men ran so fast that the devil could not catch them; and, best of all, because it gives a smack in the face to modern pseudo-scientific medical cant about hygiene, showing how the Laplanders break every 'law', human and 'divine', ventilation, bath, and diet—all the trash—and therefore enjoy the most excellent health, and live to a great old age. Still I have not succeeded in describing the immense labour there was in learning to distinguish plants on the Linnaean system. Then comes in order of time the natural system, the geographical distribution; then there is the geological relationship, so to say, to Pliocene plants, natural selection and evolution. Of that let us say nothing; let sleeping dogs lie, and evolution is a very weary dog. Most charming, however, will be found the later studies of naturalists on the interdependence of flowers and insects; there is another work the dandelion has got to do—endless, endless botany! Where did the plants come from at first? Did they come creeping up out of the sea at the edge of the estuaries, and gradually run their roots into the ground, and so make green the earth? Did Man come out of the sea, as the Greeks thought? There are so many ideas in plants. Flora, with a full lap, scattering knowledge and flowers together; everything good and sweet seems to come out of flowers, up to the very highest thoughts of the soul, and we carry them daily to the very threshold of the other world. Next you may try the microscope and its literature, and find the crystals in the rhubarb.

I remember taking sly glances when I was a very little boy at an old Culpeper's Herbal, heavily bound in leather and curiously illustrated. It was so deliciously wicked to read about the poisons; and I thought perhaps it was a book like that, only in papyrus rolls, that was used by the sorceress who got ready the poisoned mushrooms in old Rome. Youth's ideas are so imaginative, and bring together things that are so widely separated. Conscience told me I had no business to read about poisons; but there was a fearful fascination in hemlock, and I recollect tasting a little bit—it was very nasty. At this day, nevertheless, if any one wishes to begin a pleasant, interesting, unscientific acquaintance with English plants, he would do very well indeed to get a good copy of Culpeper. Grey hairs had insisted in showing themselves in my beard when, all those weary years afterwards, I thought I would like to buy the still older Englishman, Gerard, who had no Linnaeus to guide him, who walked about our English lanes centuries ago. What wonderful scenes he must have viewed when they were all a tangle of wild flowers, and plants that are now scarce were common, and the old ploughs, and the curious customs, and the wild red-deer—it would make a good picture, it really would, Gerard studying English orchids! Such a volume!—hundreds of pages, yellow of course, close type, and marvellously well printed. The minute care they must have taken in those early days of printing to get up such a book—a wonderful volume both in bodily shape and contents. Just then the only copy I could hear of was much damaged. The cunning old bookseller said he could make it up; but I have no fancy for patched books, they are not genuine; I would rather have them deficient; and the price was rather long, and so I went Gerardless. Of folk-lore and medicinal use and history and associations here you have hints. The bottom of the sack is not yet; there are the monographs, years of study expended upon one species of plant growing in one locality, perhaps; some made up into thick books and some into broad quarto pamphlets, with most beautiful plates, that, if you were to see them, would tempt you to cut them out and steal them, all sunk and lost like dead ships under the sand: piles of monographs. There are warehouses in London that are choked to the beams of the roof with them, and every fresh exploration furnishes another shelf-load. The source of the Nile was unknown a very few years ago, and now, I have no doubt, there are dozens of monographs on the flowers that flourish there. Indeed, there is not a thing that grows that may not furnish a monograph. The author spends perhaps twenty years in collecting his material, during which time he must of course come across a great variety of amusing information, and then he spends another ten years writing out a fair copy of his labours. Then he thinks it does not quite do in that form, so he snips a paragraph out of the beginning and puts it at the end; next he shifts some more matter from the middle to the preface; then he thinks it over. It seems to him that it is too big, it wants condensation. The scientific world will say he has made too much of it; it ought to read very slight, and present the facts while concealing the labour. So he sets about removing the superfluous—leaves out all the personal observations, and all the little adventures he has met with in his investigations; and so, having got it down to the dry bones and stones thereof, and omitted all the mortar that stuck them together, he sends for the engraver, and the next three years are occupied in working up the illustrations. About this time some new discovery is made by a foreign observer, which necessitates a complete revision of the subject; and so having shifted the contents of the book about hither and thither till he does not know which is the end and which is the beginning, he pitches the much-mutilated copy into a drawer and turns the key. Farewell, no more of this; his declining days shall be spent in peace. A few months afterwards a work is announced in Leipsic which 'really trenches on my favourite subject, and really after spending a lifetime I can't stand it.' By this time his handwriting has become so shaky he can hardly read it himself, so he sends in despair for a lady who works a type-writer, and with infinite patience she makes a clean manuscript of the muddled mass. To the press at last, and the proofs come rapidly. Such a relief! How joyfully easy a thing is when you set about it! but by-and-by this won't do. Sub-section A ought to be in a foot-note, family B is doubtful; and so the corrections grow and run over the margin in a thin treble hand, till they approach the bulk of the original book—a good profit for the printer; and so after about forty years the monograph is published—the work of a life is accomplished. Fifty copies are sent round to as many public libraries and learned societies, and the rest of the impression lies on the shelves till dust and time and spiders' webs have buried it. Splendid work in it too. Looked back upon from to-day with the key of modern thought, these monographs often contain a whole chest of treasure. And still there are the periodicals, a century of magazines and journals and reviews and notices that have been coming out these hundred years and dropping to the ground like dead leaves unnoticed. And then there are the art works—books about shape and colour and ornament, and a naturalist lately has been trying to see how the leaves of one tree look fitted on the boughs of another. Boundless is the wealth of Flora's lap; the ingenuity of man has been weaving wreaths out of it for ages, and still the bottom of the sack is not yet. Nor have we got much news of the dandelion. For I sit on the thrown timber under the trees and meditate, and I want something more: I want the soul of the flowers.

The bee and the butterfly take their pollen and their honey, and the strange moths so curiously coloured, like the curious colouring of the owls, come to them by night, and they turn towards the sun and live their little day, and their petals fall, and where is the soul when the body decays? I want the inner meaning and the understanding of the wild flowers in the meadow. Why are they? What end? What purpose? The plant knows, and sees, and feels; where is its mind when the petal falls? Absorbed in the universal dynamic force, or what? They make no shadow of pretence, these beautiful flowers, of being beautiful for my sake, of bearing honey for me; in short, there does not seem to be any kind of relationship between us; and yet—as I said just now—language does not express the dumb feelings of the mind any more than the flower can speak. I want to know the soul of the flowers, but the word soul does not in the smallest degree convey the meaning of my wish. It is quite inadequate; I must hope that you will grasp the drift of my meaning. All these life-laboured monographs, these classifications, works of Linnaeus, and our own classic Darwin, microscope, physiology, and the flower has not given us its message yet. There are a million books; there are no books: all the books have to be written. What a field! A whole million of books have got to be written. In this sense there are hardly a dozen of them done, and these mere primers. The thoughts of man are like the foraminifera, those minute shells which build up the solid chalk hills and lay the level plain of endless sand; so minute that, save with a powerful lens, you would never imagine the dust on your fingers to be more than dust. The thoughts of man are like these: each to him seems great in his day, but the ages roll, and they shrink till they become triturated dust, and you might, as it were, put a thousand on your thumb-nail. They are not shapeless dust for all that; they are organic, and they build and weld and grow together, till in the passage of time they will make a new earth and a new life. So I think I may say there are no books; the books are yet to be written.

Let us get a little alchemy out of the dandelions. They were not precise, the Arabian sages, with their flowing robes and handwriting; there was a large margin to their manuscripts, much imagination. Therein they failed, judged by the monograph standard, but gave a subtle food for the mind. Some of this I would fain see now inspiring the works and words of our great men of science and thought—a little alchemy. A great change is slowly going forward all over the printing-press world, I mean wherever men print books and papers. The Chinese are perhaps outside that world at present, and the other Asian races; the myriads, too, of the great southern islands and of Africa. The change is steadily, however, proceeding wherever the printing-press is used. Nor Pope, nor Kaiser, nor Czar, nor Sultan, nor fanatic monk, nor muezzin, shouting in vain from his minaret, nor, most fanatic of all, the fanatic shouting in vain in London, can keep it out—all powerless against a bit of printed paper. Bits of printed paper that listen to no command, to which none can say, 'Stand back; thou shalt not enter.' They rise on the summer whirlwinds from the very dust of the road, and float over the highest walls; they fall on the well-kept lawns—monastery, prison, palace—there is no fortress against a bit of printed paper. They penetrate where even Danaë's gold cannot go. Our Darwins, our Lyalls, Herschels, Faradays— all the immense army of those that go down to nature with considering eye— are steadfastly undermining and obliterating the superstitious past, literally burying it under endless loads of accumulated facts; and the printing-presses, like so many Argos, take these facts on their voyage round the world. Over go temples, and minarets, and churches, or rather there they stay, the hollow shells, like the snail shells which thrushes have picked clean; there they stay like Karnac, where there is no more incense, like the stone circles on our own hills, where there are no more human sacrifices. Thus men's minds all over the print-ing-press world are unlearning the falsehoods that have bound them down so long; they are unlearning, the first step to learn. They are going down to nature and taking up the clods with their own hands, and so coming to have touch of that which is real. As yet we are in the fact stage; by-and-by we shall come to the alchemy, and get the honey for the inner mind and soul. I found, therefore, from the dandelion that there were no books, and it came upon me, believe me, as a great surprise, for I had lived quite certain that I was surrounded with them. It is nothing but unlearning, I find now; five thousand books to unlearn.

Then to unlearn the first ideas of history, of science, of social institutions, to unlearn one's own life and purpose; to unlearn the old mode of thought and way of arriving at things; to take off peel after peel, and so get by degrees slowly towards the truth—thus writing as it were, a sort of floating book in the mind, almost remaking the soul. It seems as if the chief value of books is to give us something to unlearn. Sometimes I feel indignant at the false views that were instilled into me in early days, and then again I see that that very indignation gives me a moral life. I hope in the days to come future thinkers will unlearn us, and find ideas infinitely better. How marvellous it seems that there should be found communities furnished with the printing-press and fully convinced they are more intelligent than ants, and yet deliberately refus-ing by a solid 'popular' vote to accept free libraries! They look with scorn on the mediaeval times, when volumes were chained in the college library or to the desk at church. Ignorant times those! A good thing it would be if only three books were chained to a desk, open and free in every parish throughout the kingdom now. So might the wish to unlearn be at last started in the inert mind of the mass. Almost the only books left to me to read, and not to unlearn very much, are my first books—the graven classics of Greece and Rome, cut with a stylus so deeply into the tablet they cannot be erased. Little of the monograph or of classification, no bushel baskets full of facts, no minute dissection of nature, no attempt to find the soul under the scalpel. Thoughts which do not exactly deal with nature direct in a mechanical way, as the chemist labels all his gums and spices and earths in small boxes—I wonder if anybody at Athens ever made a collection of the coleoptera? Yet in some way they had got the spirit of the earth and sea, the soul of the sun. This never dies; this I wish not to unlearn; this is ever fresh and beautiful as a summer morning:—

> Such the golden crocus,
> Fair flower of early spring; the gopher white,
> And fragrant thyme, and all the unsown beauty
> Which in moist grounds the verdant meadows bear;
> The ox-eye, the sweet-smelling flower of Jove,
> The chalca, and the much-sung hyacinth,
> And the low-growing violet, to which
> Dark Proserpine a darker hue has given.

They come nearest to our own violets and cowslips—the unsown beauty of our meadows—to the hawthorn leaf and the high pinewood. I can forget all else that I have read, but it is difficult to forget these even when I will. I read them in English. I had the usual Latin and Greek instruction, but I read them in English deliberately. For the inflexion of the vowel I care nothing; I prize the idea. Scholars may regard me with scorn. I reply with equal scorn. I say that a great classic thought is greater to an English mind in English words than in any other form, and therein fits best to this our life and day. I read them in English first, and intend to do so to the end. I do not know what set me on these books, but I began them when about eighteen. The first of all was Diogenes Laertius's *Lives of the Philosophers*. It was a happy choice; my good genius, I suppose, for you see I was already fairly well read in modern science, and these old Greek philosophies set me thinking backwards, unwinding and unlearning, and getting at that eidolon which is not to be found in the mechanical heavens of this age. I still read him. I still find new things, quite new, because they are so very, very old, and quite true; and with his help I seem in a measure to look back upon our thoughts now as if I had projected myself a thousand years forward in space. An imperfect book, say the critics. I do not know about that; his short paragraphs and chapters in their imperfect state convey more freshness to the mind than the thick, laboured volumes in which modern scholarship professes to describe ancient philosophy. I prefer the imperfect original records. Neither can I read the ponderous volumes of modern history, which are nothing but words. I prefer the incomplete and shattered chronicles themselves, where the swords shine and the armour rings, and all is life though but a broken frieze. Next came Plato (it took me a long time to read Plato, and I have had to unlearn much of him) and Xenophon. Socrates' dialectic method taught me how to write, or rather how to put ideas in sequence. Sophocles, too; and last, that wonderful encyclopaedia of curious things, Athenaeus. So that I found, when the idea of the hundred best books came out, that between seventy and eighty of them had been my companions almost from boyhood, those lacking to complete the number being chiefly ecclesiastical or Continental. Indeed, some years before the hundred books were talked of, the idea had occurred to me of making up a catalogue of books that could be bought for ten pounds. In an article in the *Pall Mall Gazette* on 'The Pigeons at the British Museum' I said, "It seems as if all the books in the world—really books—can be bought for 10*l.* Man's whole thought is purchasable at that small price—for the value of a watch, of a good dog." The idea of making a 10*l.* catalogue was in my mind—I did make a rough pencil one—and I still think that a 10*l.* library is worth the notice of the publishing world. My rough list did not contain a hundred. These old books of nature and nature's mind ought to be chained up, free for every man to read in every parish. These are the only books I do not wish to unlearn, one item only excepted, which I shall not here discuss. It is curious, too, that the Greek philosophers, in the more rigid sense of science, anticipated most of the drift of modern thought. Two chapters in Aristotle might almost be printed without change as summaries of our present natural science. For the facts of nature, of course, neither one hundred books nor a 10*l.* library would be worth mentioning; say five thousand, and having read those, then go to Kew, and spend a year studying the specimens of wood only stored there, such a little slice after all of the whole. You will then believe what I have advanced, that there are no books as yet; they have got to be written; and if we pursue the idea a little further, and consider that these are all about the crude clods of life—for I often feel what a very crude and clumsy clod I am—only of the earth, a minute speck among one hundred millions of stars, how shall we write what is *there*? It is only to be written by the mind or soul, and that is why I strive so much to find what I have called the alchemy of nature. Let us not be too entirely mechanical, Baconian, and experimental only; let us let the soul hope and dream and float on these oceans of accumulated facts, and feel still greater aspiration than it has ever known since first a flint was chipped before the glaciers. Man's mind is the most important fact with which we are yet acquainted. Let us not turn then against it and deny its existence with too many brazen instruments, but remember these are but a means, and that the vast lens of the Californian refractor is but glass—it is the infinite speck upon which the ray of light will fall that is the one great fact of the universe. By the mind, without instruments, the Greeks anticipated almost all our thoughts; by-and-by, having raised ourselves up upon these huge mounds of facts, we shall begin to see still greater things; to do so we must look not at the mound under foot, but at the starry horizon.

Primrose Gold in Our Village

EVERYONE SAID how beautiful the tall arching boughs of the elms looked meeting over the road at the entrance to the village. As in the East the bazaars and all the life seem to be under domes and covers, so the entry into English country life is very often under elms like these. It is a common scene, and everyone says it is beautiful. The houses just beyond are still for the most part thatched, yet there is a certain difference in the general style of the place, if you can imagine it as an engraving before your eye. Outside the black-smith's shop there are a number of strange machines painted a staring red; things with horrible knives, a machine that would be welcomed by a Chinese executioner for cutting off feet first and hands next, and so on; things with long clawy spikes that seem to prick your eyes if you look at them; and another thing is coming that makes a tremendous groan and clank. I always shrink into a gateway if I can when a traction-engine comes by, with a sort of vague prayer to Fate that it may not burst as it passes and blow me up with all my dreams. Somehow there seems such a vast mass of dust about, the grocer's shop there (which will supply you with French wine) must be sanded with it. There is an unpleasant feeling that this dust is not good, pure road dust; if a little pinch gets up the nose it has a noisome smell. It is like desiccated sewage. A direful odour rises from a grating, and the secret is out: the place has been drained. Till then it was a healthy spot; since then there has been nothing but epi-demics. This is a common experience; it is called 'sanitation'. If you Londoners go into the country for a change be careful that you do not go to a village that has been drained. Especially take notice if there are many villas about, for they are dangerous and indicate deadly improvements. Beware of villas.

Still, there are rooks and sunshine and twenty gables to draw, and do what they will they cannot quite obliterate the old place. There is a window under a low-tiled roof with yellow stonecrop above it. Yellow wallflowers, marigolds, musk, evening primrose, crown lilies, dwarf genista, eschscholtzia—every-thing yellow. Behind the window panes the window flowers are so thick they seem to flatten themselves against the glass: some scarlet geraniums, of course, but chiefly yellow calceolarias. Close to the window there is a sort of abut-ment also tiled—perhaps it is an oven—and this, too, bears yellow stonecrop. There is a gable above, and a high narrow chimney; a very pleasant 'bit' to sketch or paint. A goldenchain tree stands in front—long pendants of yellow. All the corner seems stained with golden colour. Any stranger passing along the footpath would be sure to stop and look at it and say, 'Ah! that really is a bit of old-fashioned country life. Really genuine. Very pretty indeed.' One would suppose the people who lived there would be in the foremost ranks of everything good.

The village was made upright, but they have found out many inventions; they have invented an *élite*, and found out that they possessed a stratum of 'society'—in short, they have got a Primrose Habitation, which came in with the drains. The rolls are not open to inspection, but it is believed the clergy-man and the curate belong to the *élite*—that is, to the Habitation. The old doctor certainly does—a genuine old Tory. The new doctor did not at first, but he found he had better do so afterwards, and he finds it better also to be very regular at the 'celebrations' at the church. The old doctor has spread about an idea among the old maids that the new man, who is very clever, is a dreadful materialist. In the Middle Ages if a man was very clever in chemistry he was supposed to be a necromancer and keep a familiar spirit in the neck of an alembic. To-day, if a man is very clever, there is always a suspicion that he is a wicked materialist, and deals with 'spores', and 'germs', and 'microbes'. There are no spores in the gospel. The professional tradesman, that is to say, the chemist, who is at least a hundred degrees higher in the scale than the old grocer, is thought to be on the list. There are four or five people retired, pos-sibly unprofessional tradesmen once, living in the old farmhouses that have been villafied, who are imagined to supply a good deal of the sinews of war. Of course all the upper class of Tory farmers are affiliated in some way, and there are one or two county families, the M.P. of the district, and four or five of his more or less titled friends, honorary subscribers, and several semi-county families, neither farmers, gentlemen, nor lords. The bulk of the work, however, is got through by a sort of quasi-secretary, who does all the calls and three-line whips, and arranges the meetings and carries out every-thing, and who is casually alluded to by the big folk as a 'very good fellow, you know; don't know what we should do without him,' but they don't ask him to dinner. This is very nearly all that is known by the vulgar of the vil-lage caucus, for such it is—for ways that are 'dark and tricks that are vain', commend me to the heathen Tory. There is a still darker branch of this mys-terious craft—it is the ladies, great Dames, to whom be honour and glory. What they do I do not know, but there are whispers that there are social divi-sions, and that one Dame is greater than another Dame, inasmuch that if a great Dame, one of the big folk, proposes a resolution, the resolution is car-ried, but if a lesser Dame makes a resolution it falls to the ground. Hence it appears that there are heartburnings among the angels. Still, they belong to the order of the *élite*, and the discipline is perfect.

Now a local village is a very local place. There is no very great variety of streets, no Charing Cross, no floating population that drifts up the Strand in endless stream, that drops in at a shop and buys a cigarette for a penny or an ormolu clock for seven guineas. The same customer is never seen again there, but to-morrow a fresh one takes his place. In the local village the customers are always the same. They are a fixed quantity; a glass is full of water and you cannot put any more in, there are so many beads on a string, and count them as many times as you like they are still the same number. Pictorially thus: the old grocer, who is not a 'professional tradesman', who exposes dirty Radical prints in his window for sale, who said several hard words to the clergyman a few years ago for refusing to bury his Nonconformist baby, who is a regular old sanded brute—is not boycotted. Certainly not. No private notice sent round, or placards stuck up remarking that if you deal there you will get lead pepper. Still it is not necessary to buy there if the 'professional' tradesman's brother sets up another shop. It is not that you shall not go to the old grocer, but it is suggested how much better it would be to go to the other one and so encourage him. The caucus does not say you shall not deal here; the caucus says you *shall* deal *there*. It is boycotting reversed. By-and-by the doctors found out that the prevalence of disease was due to there not being sufficient air-holes to the drains; so in making these improvements one was casually opened by the old grocer's shop. Always a beastly Radical effluvia just there. Don't stop there—spores, germs, pah! The old gentleman has written letters about it, but somehow the official wheels don't move. *Ex-officio* people are plentiful on country boards, and they are mostly heathen Tories.

A man who lives in the cottage with the beautiful flowery window was once the dog in the village with a bad name. He is a little owner, a little occupier, he has a little dairy and a little poultry farm, and a heavy mortgage. He was a shocking Radical and upset everything; he was so rough he did not care for threats of action for libel or slander; he did not care if he did go to gaol— a man fearfully and wonderfully made in contempt of authority. Mostly he cursed a good deal, especially about a green and succulent meadow with a pond of never-failing water next to his own arid and waterless fields. This meadow and pond was part of the glebe land, and the clergyman would not let it to such a drunken reprobate. By-and-by, when the Habitation was formed and Primrose gold began to work its way, some one whispered a whisper, and the pond and the meadow were placed at the disposal of this dreadful fellow. He is now shaven and wears a clean smock frock and goes to church a' Sundays. Next the villa folk came down to buy his beautiful butter and make much of his wife, a very respectable woman with a fancy for flowers—a very nice pot came down now and then from the greenhouses. Next it was found out that one of the dry and arid fields was very level and would make an excellent tennis ground for the Primrose Club. Accordingly a square acre or so was rented at a liberal price, and now you may see the stately Knights and Dames disporting where once did grow the weeds of treason rank.

Once now and then a real lord or a real lady who happens to be visiting one of the county families is marched round to the cottages and takes off his hat and says a few words about the crops, or perhaps my lady strokes the cat. This is not boycotting, it is Primrosing. The golden party work by finding out the soft places, and by making things very pleasant for those who will come under its wings. The voice of the reprobate is still, and the heart of the enemy is broken. The cobbler was another horror; he was consumptive too—evidently a judgement on the wretched atheist. The curate could do nothing with him, till by-and-by he had a great inspiration. "He wants encouragement," said the curate. The caucus thought so too. After this, about forty pairs of boots came floating in, gentlemen's and ladies' boots, neat repairs wanted, 2s. 6d., 3s. 6d. each. By-and-by the curate said "You have got a dreadful cough," and the upshot was they sent him to the seaside for a month, and when he came back his cough was gone and also many of his ancient prejudices. He had no further objection to any number of half-crowns—another vote secure.

Primrosing goes a great deal higher than cobblers and dairymen. If you are pliant and flexible and don't mind being petted you have nice things put in your way, and you are passed, not only in the local village, but right up to London if you want to do business there. If you are not pliant, you are not harrowed, but you are not watered, and it is best to get out of the local village. Then there are decorations, and the *élite* of the Dames wear Special Service brooches. What these mysterious special services are, no one knows. Certain, however, it is that a powerful caucus is being established everywhere throughout the country, and the same style of thing is carried on where there is not a formal Habitation.

My Old Village

"JOHN BROWN is dead," said an aged friend and visitor in answer to my inquiry for the strong labourer.

"Is he really dead?" I asked, for it seemed impossible.

"He is. He came home from his work in the evening as usual, and seemed to catch his foot in the threshold and fell forward on the floor. When they picked him up he was dead."

I remember the doorway; a raised piece of wood ran across it, as is commonly the case in country cottages, such as one might easily catch one's foot against if one did not notice it; but he knew that bit of wood well. The floor was of brick, hard to fall on and die. He must have come down over the crown of the hill, with his long slouching stride, as if his legs had been half pulled away from his body by his heavy boots in the furrows when a ploughboy. He must have turned up the steps in the bank to his cottage, and so, touching the threshold, ended. He is gone through the great doorway, and one pencil-mark is rubbed out. There used to be a large hearth in that room, a larger room than in most cottages; and when the fire was lit, and the light shone on the yellowish red brick beneath and the large rafters overhead, it was homely and pleasant. In summer the door was always wide open. Close by on the high bank there was a spot where the first wild violets came. You might look along miles of hedgerow, but there were never any until they had shown by John Brown's.

If a man's work that he has done all the days of his life could be collected and piled up around him in visible shape, what a vast mound there would be beside some! If each act or stroke was represented, say by a brick, John Brown would have stood the day before his ending by the side of a monument as high as a pyramid. Then if in front of him could be placed the sum and product of his labour, the profit to himself, he could have held it in his clenched hand like a nut, and no one would have seen it. Our modern people think they train their sons to strength by football and rowing and jumping, and what are called athletic exercises; all of which it is the fashion now to preach as very noble, and likely to lead to the goodness of the race. Certainly feats are accomplished and records are beaten, but there is no real strength gained, no hardihood built up. Without hardihood it is of little avail to be able to jump an inch farther than somebody else. Hardihood is the true test, hardihood is the ideal, and not these caperings or ten minutes' spurts.

Now, the way they made the boy John Brown hardy was to let him roll about on the ground with naked legs and bare head from morn till night, from June till December, from January till June. The rain fell on his head, and he played in wet grass to his knees. Dry bread and a little lard was his chief food. He went to work while he was still a child. At half-past three in the morning he was on his way to the farm stables, there to help feed the cart-horses, which used to be done with great care very early in the morning. The carter's whip used to sting his legs, and sometimes he felt the butt. At fifteen he was no taller than the sons of well-to-do people at eleven; he scarcely seemed to grow at all till he was eighteen or twenty, and even then very slowly, but at last became a tall big man. That slouching walk, with knees always bent, diminished his height to appearance; he really was the full size, and every inch of his frame had been slowly welded together by this ceaseless work, continual life in the open air, and coarse hard food. This is what makes a man hardy. This is what makes a man able to stand almost anything, and gives a power of endurance that can never be obtained by any amount of gymnastic training.

I used to watch him mowing with amazement. Sometimes he would begin at half-past two in the morning, and continue till night. About eleven o'clock, which used to be the mowers' noon, he took a rest on a couch of half-dried grass in the shade of the hedge. For the rest, it was mow, mow, mow for the long summer day.

John Brown was dead: died in an instant at his cottage door. I could hardly credit it, so vivid was the memory of his strength. The gap of time since I had seen him last had made no impression on me; to me he was still in my mind the John Brown of the hayfield; there was nothing between then and his death.

He used to catch us boys the bats in the stable, and tell us fearful tales of the ghosts he had seen; and bring the bread from the town in an old-fashioned wallet, half in front and half behind, long before the bakers' carts began to come round in country places. One evening he came into the dairy carrying a yoke of milk, staggering, with tipsy gravity; he was quite sure he did not want any assistance, he could pour the milk into the pans. He tried, and fell at full length and bathed himself from head to foot. Of later days they say he worked in the town a good deal, and did not look so well or so happy as on the farm. In this cottage opposite the violet bank they had small-pox once, the only case I recollect in the hamlet—the old men used to say everybody had it when they were young; this was the only case in my time, and they recovered quickly without any loss, nor did the disease spread. A roomy wellbuilt cottage like that, on dry ground, isolated, is the only hospital worthy of the name. People have a chance to get well in such places; they have very great difficulty in the huge buildings that are put up expressly for them. I have a Convalescent Home in my mind at the moment, a vast building. In these great blocks what they call ventilation is a steady draught, and there is no 'home' about it. It is all walls and regulations and draughts, and altogether miserable. I would infinitely rather see any friend of mine in John Brown's cottage. That terrible disease, however, seemed to quite spoil the violet bank opposite, and I never picked one there afterwards. There is something in disease so destructive, as it were, to flowers.

The hundreds of times I saw the tall chimney of that cottage rise out of the hill-side as I came home at all hours of the day and night! the first chimney after a long journey, always comfortable to see, especially so in earlier days, when we had a kind of halting belief in John Brown's ghosts, several of which were dotted along that road according to him. The ghosts die as we grow older, they die and their places are taken by real ghosts. I wish I had sent John Brown a pound or two when I was in good health; but one is selfish then, and puts off things till it is too late—a lame excuse verily. I can scarcely believe now that he is really dead, gone as you might casually pluck a hawthorn leaf from the hedge.

The next cottage was a very marked one, for houses grow to their owners. The low thatched roof had rounded itself and stooped down to fit itself to Job's shoulders; the walls had got short and thick to suit him, and they had a yellowish colour, like his complexion, as if chewing tobacco had stained his cheeks right through. Tobacco juice had likewise penetrated and tinted the wall. It was cut off as it seemed by a party-wall into one room, instead of which there were more rooms beyond which no one would have suspected. Job had a way of shaking hands with you with his right hand, while his left hand was casually doing something else in a detached sort of way. "Yes, sir," and "No, sir," and nodding to everything you said all so complaisant, but at the end of the bargain you generally found yourself a few shillings in some roundabout manner on the wrong side. Job had a lot of shut-up rooms in his house and in his character, which never seemed to be opened to daylight. The eaves hung over and beetled like his brows, and he had a forelock, a regular antique forelock, which he used to touch with the greatest humility. There was a long bough of an elm hanging over one gable just like the forelock. His face was a blank, like the broad end wall of the cottage, which had no window—at least you might think so until you looked up and discovered one little arrow slit, one narrow pane, and woke with a start to the idea that Job was always up there watching and listening. That was how he looked out of his one eye so intensely cunning, the other being a wall eye—that is, the world supposed so, as he kept it half shut, always between the lights; but whether it was really blind or not I cannot say. Job caught rats and rabbits and moles, and bought fagots or potatoes, or fruit or rabbit-skins, or rusty iron: wonderful how he seemed to have command of money. It was done probably by buying and selling almost simultaneously, so that the cash passed really from one customer to another, and was never his at all. Also he worked as a labourer, chiefly piece-work; also Mrs. Job had a shop window about two feet square: snuff and tobacco, bread and cheese, immense big round jumbles and sugar, kept on the floor above, and reached down by hand, when wanted, through the opening for the ladder stairs. The front door—Job's right hand—was always open in summer, and the flagstones of the floor chalked round their edges; a clean table, clean chairs, decent crockery, an old clock about an hour slow, a large hearth with a minute fire to boil the kettle without heating the room. Tea was usually at half-past three, and it is a fact that many well-to-do persons, as they came along the road hot and dusty, used to drop in and rest and take a cup— very little milk and much gossip. Two paths met just there, and people used to step in out of a storm of rain, a sort of thatched house club. Job was somehow on fair terms with nearly everybody, and that is a wonderful thing in a village, where everybody knows everybody's business, and petty interests continually cross. The strangest fellow and the strangest way of life, and yet I do not believe a black mark was ever put against him; the shiftiness was all for nothing. It arose, no doubt, out of the constant and eager straining to gain a little advantage and make an extra penny. Had Job been a Jew he would have been rich. He was the exact counterpart of the London Jew dealer, set down in the midst of the country. Job should have been rich. Such immense dark brown jumbles, such cheek-distenders—never any French sweetmeats or chocolate or bonbons to equal these. I really think I could eat one now. The pennies and fourpenny bits—there were fourpenny bits in those days—that went behind that two-foot window, goodness! there was no end. Job used to chink them in a pint pot sometimes before the company, to give them an idea of his great hoards. He always tried to impress people with his wealth, and would talk of a fifty-pound contract as if it was nothing to him. Jumbles are eternal, if nothing else is. I thought then there was not such another shop as Job's in the universe. I have found since that there is a Job shop in every village, and in every street in every town—that is to say, a window for jumbles and rubbish; and if you don't know it, you may be quite sure your children do, and spend many a sly penny there. Be as rich as you may, and give them gilded sweetmeats at home, still they will slip round to the Job shop.

It was a pretty cottage, well backed with trees and bushes, with a south-east mixture of sunlight and shade, and little touches that cannot be suggested by writing. Job had not got the Semitic instinct of keeping. The art of acquisition he possessed to some extent, that was his right hand; but somehow the half-crowns slipped away through his unstable left hand, and fortune was a greasy pole to him. His left hand was too cunning for him, it wanted to manage things too cleverly. If it had only had the Semitic grip, digging the nails into the flesh to hold tight each separate coin, he would have been village rich. The great secret is the keeping. Finding is by no means keeping. Job did not flourish in his old days; the people changed round about. Job is gone, and I think every one of that cottage is either dead or moved. Empty.

The next cottage was the water-bailiff's, who looked after the great pond or 'broad'. There were one or two old boats, and he used to leave the oars leaning against a wall at the side of the house. These oars looked like fragments of a wreck, broken and irregular. The right-hand scull was heavy, as if made of ironwood, the blade broad and spoon-shaped, so as to have a most powerful grip of the water. The left-hand scull was light and slender, with a narrow blade like a marrow scoop; so when you had the punt, you had to pull very hard with your left hand and gently with the right to get the forces equal. The punt had a list of its own, and no matter how you rowed, it would still make leeway. Those who did not know its character were perpetually trying to get this crooked wake straight, and consequently went round and round exactly like the whirligig beetle. Those who knew used to let the leeway proceed a good way and then alter it, so as to act in the other direction like an elongated zigzag. These sculls the old fellow would bring you as if they were great treasures, and watch you off in the punt as if he was parting with his dearest. At that date it was no little matter to coax him round to unchain his vessel. You had to take an interest in the garden, in the baits, and the weather, and be very humble; then perhaps he would tell you he did not want it for the trimmers, or the withy, or the flags, and you might have it for an hour as far as he could see; 'did not think my lord's steward would come over that morning; of course, if he did you must come in,' and so on; and if the stars were propitious, by-and-by the punt was got afloat. These sculls were tilted up against the wall, and as you innocently went to take one, Wauw!—a dirty little ill-tempered mongrel poodle rolled himself like a ball to your heels and snapped his teeth—Wauw! At the bark, out rushed the old lady, his housekeeper, shouting in the shrillest key to the dog to lie still, and to you that the bailiff would be there in a minute. At the sound of her shrewish 'yang-yang' down came the old man from the bank, and so one dog fetched out the lot. The three were exactly alike somehow. Beside these diamond sculls he had a big gun, with which he used to shoot the kingfishers that came for the little fish; the number he slaughtered was very great; he persecuted them as

Domitian did the flies: he declared that a kingfisher would carry off a fish heavier than itself. Also he shot rooks, once now and then strange wild fowl with this monstrous iron pipe, and something happened with this gun one evening which was witnessed, and after that the old fellow was very benevolent, and the punt was free to one or two who knew all about it. There is an old story about the stick that would not beat the dog, and the dog would not bite the pig, and so on; and so I am quite sure that ill-natured cur could never have lived with that 'yang-yang' shrew, nor could any one else but he have turned the gear of the hatch, nor have endured the dog and the woman, and the constant miasma from the stagnant waters. No one else could have shot anything with that cumbrous weapon, and no one else could row that punt straight. He used to row it quite straight, to the amazement of a wondering world, and somehow supplied the motive force—the stick—which kept all these things going. He is gone, and, I think, the housekeeper too, and the house has had several occupants since, who have stamped down the old ghosts and thrust them out of doors.

After this the cottages and houses came in little groups, some up crooked lanes, hidden away by elms as if out of sight in a cupboard, and some dotted along the brooks, scattered so that, unless you had connected them all with a very long rope, no stranger could have told which belonged to the village and which did not. They drifted into various tithings, and yet it was all the same place. They were all thatched. It was a thatched village. This is strictly accurate and strictly inaccurate, for I think there were one or two tiled and one 'slated', and perhaps a modern one slated. Nothing is ever quite rigid or complete that is of man; all rules have a chip in them. The way they built the older thatched farmhouses was to put up a very high wall in front and a very low one behind, and then the roof in a general way sloped down from the high wall to the low wall, an acre broad of thatch. These old thatched houses seemed to be very healthy so long as the old folk lived in them in the old-fashioned way. Thatch is believed to give an equable temperature. The air blew all round them, and it might be said all through them; for the front door was always open three parts of the year, and at the back the dairies were in a continual blow. Upstairs the houses were only one room thick, so that each wall was an outside wall, or rather it was a wall one side and thatched the other, so that the wind went through if a window was open. Modem houses are often built two rooms thick, so that the air does not circulate from one side to the other. No one seemed to be ill, unless he brought it home with him from some place where he had been visiting. The diseases they used to have were long-lived, such as rheumatism, which may keep a man comfortably in aches and pains forty years. My dear old friend, however, taking them one by one, went through the lot and told me of the ghosts. The forefathers I knew are all gone—the stout man, the lame man, the paralysed man, the gruff old stick: not one left. There is not one left of the old farmers, not a single one. The fathers, too, of our own generation have been dropping away. The strong young man who used to fill us with such astonishment at the feats he would achieve without a thought, no gymnastic training, to whom a sack of wheat was a toy. The strong young man went one day into the harvest-field, as he had done so many times before. Suddenly he felt a little dizzy. By-and-by he went home and became very ill with sunstroke; he recovered, but he was never strong again; he gradually declined for twelve months, and next harvest-time he was under the daisies. Just one little touch of the sun, and the strength of man faded as a leaf. The hardy dark young man, built of iron, broad, thick, and short, who looked as if frost, snow, and heat were all the same to him, had something go wrong in his lung: one twelvemonth, and there was an end. This was a very unhappy affair. The pickaxe and the spade have made almost a full round to every door; I do not want to think any more about this. Family changes and the pressure of these hard times have driven out most of the rest; some seem to have quite gone out of sight; some have crossed the sea; some have abandoned the land as a livelihood. Of the few, the very few that still remain, still fewer abide in their original homes. Time has shuffled them about from house to house like a pack of cards. Of them all, I verily believe there is but one soul living in the same old house. If the French had landed in the mediaeval way to harry with fire and sword, they could not have swept the place more clean.

Almost the first thing I did with pen and ink as a boy was to draw a map of the hamlet with the roads and lanes and paths, and I think some of the ponds, and with each of the houses marked and the occupier's name. Of course it was very roughly done, and not to any scale, yet it was perfectly accurate and full of detail. I wish I could find it, but the confusion of time has scattered and mixed these early papers. A map by Ptolemy would bear as much resemblance to the same country in a modern atlas as mine to the present state of that locality. It is all gone—rubbed out. The names against the whole of those houses have been altered, one only excepted, and changes have taken place there. Nothing remains. This is not in a century, half a century, or even in a quarter of a century, but in a few ticks of the clock.

I think I have heard that the oaks are down. They may be standing or down, it matters nothing to me; the leaves I last saw upon them are gone for evermore, nor shall I ever see them come there again ruddy in spring. I would not see them again even if I could; they could never look again as they used to do. There are too many memories there. The happiest days become the saddest

afterwards; let us never go back, lest we too die. There are no such oaks anywhere else, none so tall and straight, and with such massive heads, on which
the sun used to shine as if on the globe of the earth, one side in shadow, the
other in bright light. How often I have looked at oaks since, and yet have never
been able to get the same effect from them! Like an old author printed in
another type, the words are the same, but the sentiment is different. The
brooks have ceased to run. There is no music now at the old hatch where we
used to sit in danger of our lives, happy as kings, on the narrow bar over the
deep water. The barred pike that used to come up in such numbers are no
more among the flags. The perch used to drift down the stream, and then
bring up again. The sun shone there for a very long time, and the water rippled and sang, and it always seemed to me that I could feel the rippling and
the singing and the sparkling back through the centuries. The brook is dead,
for when man goes nature ends. I dare say there is water there still but it is not
the brook; the brook is gone like John Brown's soul. There used to be clouds
over the fields, white clouds in blue summer skies. I have lived a good deal on
clouds; they have been meat to me often; they bring something to the spirit
which even the trees do not. I see clouds now sometimes when the iron grip of
hell permits for a minute or two; they are very different clouds, and speak differently. I long for some of the old clouds that had no memories. There were
nights in those times over those fields, not darkness, but Night, full of glowing suns and glowing richness of life that sprang up to meet them. The nights
are there still; they are everywhere, nothing local in the night; but it is not the
Night to me seen through the window.

There used to be footpaths. Following one of them, the first field always
had a good crop of grass; over the next stile there was a great oak standing
alone in the centre of the field, generally a great cart-horse under it, and a few
rushes scattered about the furrows; the fourth was always full of the forest
clover; in the fifth you could scent the beans on the hill, and there was a hedge
like a wood, and a nest of the long-tailed tit; the sixth had a runnel and blue
forget-me-nots; the seventh had a brooklet and scattered trees along it; from
the eighth you looked back on the slope and saw the thatched houses you had
left behind under passing shadows, and rounded white clouds going straight
for the distant hills, each cloud visibly bulging and bowed down like a bag. I
cannot think how the distant thatched houses came to stand out with such
clear definition and etched outline and bluish shadows; and beyond these was
the uncertain vale that had no individuality, but the trees put their arms
together and became one. All these were meadows, every step was among
grass, beautiful grass, and the cuckoos sang as if they had found paradise. A
hundred years ago a little old man with silver buckles on his shoes used to

walk along this footpath once a week in summer, taking his children over to drink milk at the farm; but though he set them every time to note the number of fields, so busy were they with the nests and the flowers, they could never be sure at the end of the journey whether there were eight or nine. To make quite sure at last, he took with them a pocket full of apples, one of which was eaten in each field, and so they came to know for certain that the number of meadows was either eight or nine, I forget which; and so you see this great experiment did not fix the faith of mankind. Like other great truths, it has grown dim, but it seems strange to think how this little incident could have been borne in mind for a century. There was another footpath that led through the peewit field, where the green plovers for evermore circle round in spring; then past the nightingale field, by the largest maple trees that grew in that country; this too was all grass. Another led along the water to bluebell land; another into the coombs of the hills; all meadows, which was the beauty of it; for though you could find wheat in plenty if you liked, you always walked in grass. All round the compass you could still step on sward. This is rare. Of one other path I have a faded memory, like a silk marker in an old book; in truth, I don't want to remember it except the end of it where it came down to the railway. So full was the mind of romance in those days, that I used to get there specially in time to see the express go up, the magnificent engine of the broad gauge that swept along with such ease and power to London. I wish I could feel like that now. The feeling is not quite gone even now, and I have often since seen these great broad-gauge creatures moving alive to and fro like Ezekiel's wheel dream beside the platforms of Babylon with much of the same old delight. Still I never went back with them to the faded footpath. They are all faded now, these footpaths.

The walnut trees are dead at home. They gave such a thick shade when the fruit was juicy ripe, and the hoods cracked as they fell; they peeled as easily as taking off a glove; the sweetest and nuttiest of fruit. It was delicious to sit there with a great volume of Sir Walter Scott, half in sunshine, half in shade, dreaming of 'Kenilworth' and Wayland Smith's cave; only the difficulty was to balance the luxuries, when to peel the walnuts and when to read the book, and how to adjust oneself to perfection so as to get the exact amount of sunshine and shadow. Too much luxury. There was a story, too, told by one Abu-Kaka ibn Ja'is, of the caravan that set forth in 1483 to cross the desert, and being overwhelmed by a sandstorm, lost their way. They wandered for some time till hunger and thirst began to consume them, and then suddenly lit on an oasis unknown to the oldest merchant of Baghdad. There they found refreshing waters and palms and a caravanserai; and, what was most pleasant, the people at the bazaar and the prince hastened to fill them with hospitality; sheep were killed, and kids were roasted, and all was joy. They were not permitted to depart till they had feasted, when they set out again on their journey, and each at leaving was presented with strings of pearls and bags of rubies, so that at last they came home with all the magnificence of kings. They found, however, that instead of having been absent only a month or two they had been gone twenty years, so swiftly had time sped. As they grew old, and their beards grey, and their frames withered, and the pearls were gone, and the rubies spent, they said, "We will go back to the city of the oasis." They set out, each on his camel, one lame, the other paralytic, and the third blind, but still the way was plain, for had they not trodden it before? and they had with them the astrolabe of the astronomer that fixes the track by the stars. Time wore on, and presently the camels' feet brought them nearer and nearer the wished-for spot. One saw the water, and another the palms, but when they came near, it was the mirage, and deep sand covered the place. Then they separated, and each hastened home; but the blind had no leader, and the lame fell from his camel, and the paralytic had no more dates, and their whited bones have disappeared.* Many another tale, too, I read under the trees that are gone like human beings. Sometimes I went forth to the nooks in the deep meadows by the hazel mounds, and some-times I parted the ash-tree wands. In my waistcoat pocket I had a little red book, made square; I never read it out of doors, but I always carried it in my pocket till it was frayed and the binding broken; the smallest of red books, but very much therein—the poems and sonnets of Mr. William Shakespeare. Some books are alive. The book I have still, it cannot die; the ash copses are cut, and the hazel mounds destroyed.

Was every one, then, so pleasant to me in those days? were the people all so beneficent and kindly that I must needs look back; all welcoming with open hand and open door? No, the reverse; there was not a single one friendly to me. Still that has nothing to do with it; I never thought about them, and I am quite certain they never thought about me. They are all gone, and there is an end. Incompatibility would describe our connection best. Nothing to do with them at all; it was me. I planted myself everywhere—in all the fields and under the trees. The curious part of it is that though they are all dead, and

---

* The Arabian commentator thinks this story a myth: the oasis in the desert is the time of youth, which passes so quickly, and is not recognized till it is gone; the pearls and rubies, the joys of love, which make the fortunate lover as a king. In old age every man is afflicted with disease or infirmity, every one is paralytic, lame, or blind. They set out to find a second youth—the dream of immortality—with the astrolabe, which is the creed or Koran all take as their guide. And death separated the company. This is only his pragmatic way; the circumstance is doubtless historic.

'worms have eaten them, but not for love,' we continually meet them in other shapes. We say, 'Holloa, here is old So-and-so coming; that is exactly his jaw, that's his Flemish face;' or, 'By Jove, yonder is So-and-so; that's his very walk:' one almost expects them to speak as one meets them in the street. There seem to be certain set types which continually crop up again whithersoever you go, and even certain tricks of speech and curves of the head—a set of family portraits walking about the world. It was not the people, neither for good, for evil, nor indifference.

I planted myself everywhere under the trees in the fields and footpaths, by day and by night, and that is why I have never put myself into the charge of the many wheeled creatures that move on the rails and gone back thither, lest I might find the trees look small, and the elms mere switches, and the fields shrunken, and the brooks dry, and no voice anywhere. Nothing but my own ghost to meet me by every hedge. I fear lest I should find myself more dead than all the rest. And verily I wish, could it be without injury to others, that the sand of the desert would rise and roll over and obliterate the place for ever and ever.

I need not wish, for I have been conversing again with learned folk about this place, and they begin to draw my view to certain considerations. These very learned men point out to me a number of objections, for the question they sceptically put is this: are you quite certain that such a village ever existed? In the first place, they say, you have only got one other witness beside yourself, and she is aged, and has defective sight; and really we don't know what to say to accepting such evidence unsupported. Secondly, John Brown cannot be found to bear testimony. Thirdly, there are no ghosts there; that can be demonstrated. It renders a case unsubstantial to introduce these flimsy spirits. Fourthly, the map is lost, and it might be asked was there ever such a map? Fifthly, the people are all gone. Sixthly, no one ever saw any particular sparkle on the brook there, and the clouds appear to be of the same commonplace order that go about everywhere. Seventhly, no one can find these footpaths, which probably led nowhere; and as for the little old man with silver buckles on his shoes, it is a story only fit for someone in his dotage. You can't expect grave and considerate men to take your story as it stands; they must consult the Ordnance Survey and Domesday Book; and the fact is, you have not got the shadow of a foundation on which to carry your case into court. I may resent this, but I cannot deny that the argument is very black against me, and I begin to think that my senses have deceived me. It is as they say. No one else seems to have seen the sparkle on the brook, or heard the music at the hatch, or to have felt back through the centuries; and when I try to describe these things to them they look at me with stolid incredulity. No one seems to understand how I got food from the clouds, nor what there was in the night, nor why it is not so good to look at it out of window. They turn their faces away from me, so that perhaps after all I was mistaken, and there never was any such place or any such meadows, and I was never there. And perhaps in course of time I shall find out also, when I pass away physically, that as a matter of fact there never was any earth.

Absence of Design in Nature

IN THE PARLOUR to which I have retired from the heat there is a chair and a table, and a picture on the wall: the chair was made for an object and a purpose, to sit in; the table for a purpose, to write on; the picture was painted for a purpose, to please the eye. But outside, in the meadow, in the hedge, on the hill, in the water; or, looking still farther, to the sun, the moors, and stars, I see no such chair, or table, or picture.

Pondering deeply and for long upon the plants, the living things (myself, too, as a physical being): upon the elements, on the holy miracle, water; the holy miracle, sunlight; the earth, and the air, I come at last—and not without, for a while, sorrow—to the inevitable conclusion that there is no object, no end, no purpose, no design, and no plan; no anything, that is.

By a strong and continued effort, I compelled myself to see the world mentally: with my mind, as it were, abstracted; hold yourself, as it were, apart from it, and there is no object, and no plan; no law, and no rule.

From childhood we build up for ourselves an encyclopaedia of the world, answering all questions: we turn to Day, and the reply is Light; to Night, and the reply is Darkness. It is difficult to burst through these fetters and to get beyond Day and Night: but, in truth, there is no Day and Night; the sun always shines. It is our minds which supply the purpose, the end, the plan, the law, and the rule. For the practical matters of life, these are sufficient— they are like conventional agreements. But if you wish to really know the truth, there is none. When you first realize this, the whole arch of thought falls in; the structure the brain has reared, or, rather, which so many minds have reared for it, becomes a crumbling ruin, and there seems nothing left. I felt crushed when I first saw that there was no chair, no table, no picture, in nature: I use 'nature' in the widest sense; in the cosmos then. Nothing especially made for man to sit on, to write on, to admire—not even the colour of the buttercups or the beautiful sun-gleam which had me spellbound glowing on the water in my hand in the rocky cell.

The rudest quern ever yet discovered in which the earliest man ground his wheat did not fall from the sky; even that poor instrument, the mere hollowed stone, was not thrown to him prepared for use; he had to make it himself. There neither is, nor has been, nor will be any chair, or table, or picture, or quern in the cosmos. Nor is there any plan even in the buttercups themselves, looked at for themselves: they are not geometrical, or mathematical; nor precisely circular, nor anything regular. A general pattern, as a common colour, may be claimed for them, a pattern, however, liable to modification under cultivation; but, fully admitting this, it is no more than saying that water is water: that one crystal is always an octahedron, another a dodecahedron; that one element is oxygen and another hydrogen; that the earth is the earth; and the sun, the sun. It is only stating in the simplest way the fact that a thing *is*: and, after the most rigid research, that is, in the end, all that can be stated.

To say that there is a general buttercup pattern is only saying that it is not a bluebell or violet. Perhaps the general form of the buttercup is not absolutely necessary to its existence; many birds can fly equally well if their tails be removed, or even a great part of their wings. There are some birds that do not fly at all. Some further illustrations presently will arise; indeed, nothing could be examined without affording some. I had forgotten that the parlour, beside the chair and table, had a carpet. The carpet has a pattern: it is woven; the threads can be discerned, and a little investigation shows beyond doubt that it was designed and made by a man. It is certainly pretty and ingenious. But the grass of my golden meadow has no design, and no purpose: it is beautiful, and more; it is divine.

When at last I had disabused my mind of the enormous imposture of a design, an object, and an end, a purpose or a system, I began to see dimly how much more grandeur, beauty and hope there is in a divine chaos—not chaos in the sense of disorder or confusion but simply the absence of order—than there is in a universe made by pattern. This draught-board universe my mind had laid out: this machine-made world and piece of mechanism; what a petty, despicable, microcosmos I had substituted for the reality.

Logically, that which has a design or a purpose has a limit. The very idea of a design or a purpose has since grown repulsive to me, on account of its littleness. I do not venture, for a moment, even to attempt to supply a reason to take the place of the exploded plan. I simply deliberately deny, or, rather, I have now advanced to that stage that to my own mind even the admission of the subject to discussion is impossible. I look at the sunshine and feel that there is no contracted order: there is divine chaos, and, in it, limitless hope and possibilities.

From Notebook XXII, February 1887

SL. IT IS EASY to write upon that which is already written, to analyse criticise enlarge; it is another thing to go at once to nature & the immense out of doors, & try to write from that, I sit & ponder in the sun & ponder & still ponder & cannot even express the magnitude of the problem the vastness of the thought that comes.

It is difficult to realize that all is as beautiful now as at Coate—yet it is.

. . .

SL. Every day from the moment I see the light I have to go over my thoughts again. This is the peculiarity of studying from the sun.

SL. If life were immortal still I should think there were other ideas & the Idea Beyond.

SL. *** All ends &n begins & is comprised in *life* now and describing that closest comes nearest the thought I have to give. It is that really.

. . .

SL. *** Yet *all* supernatural [. . .] in the whole idea.

SL. If no* Beyond—how then this *now*?

SL. I seem to be beginning the great task of life now I am so mutilated—eye weak, nictitating, confined to narrow circle, hopes broken like limbs.

. . .

I feel that I know nothing more than when I began to think & be conscious— say at 15.

. . .

SL. Sun Life. To lean against the fir & feel it [become?] air.

. . .

SL. In youth sucked the egg of the world dry—now the fragments of the shell among my teeth.

While we think only of the earth the idea of a beginning comes & seems absolutely necessary. When we find the immensity of the universe then the idea of a beginning vanishes & the idea of constant existence takes its place.

. . .

***SL. Matter not despicable not dead—Is there any dead matter?

. . .

SL. Everything formed of matter—lichen, polyp, plant, beautiful flower, the prismatic feathers of the starling, ourselves, the eye, the brain, memory, the bones of lime, ie glowing & living stone & where does life pass into [. . .]. Consider the thumbnail, which you can cut without pain (the quick at the root). No more feeling than brass stair-rod. Blackbird entirely formed of matter—eye, mind, heart, love, song. All formed *of* matter: then also *by* matter, of itself, of its own inherent quality—spontaneous generation, and so man and his mind. Now analyse matter and it resolves to force and force to still subtler suggestions. And matter analysed is found to be full of intelligence. It resolves into mind. If therefore matter is capable of itself forming the mind of man, under different conditions in other regions it may form other forms of intelligence. Upon analysis therefore it seems as if that into which the body after is resolved is itself life, is itself intelligence (as matter in its subtler form is mind) (coming to this conclusion on purely materialistic grounds).

Each grain or particle of matter seems to have the latent possibility in it of becoming mind. Every grain of seed or dust may some day be a thought in some man's brain.

It is the property of matter to turn to or become life [sand?] intelligent (as oyster). As much a property of matter as weight.

As humus quickest turns to grain again perhaps intelligence quickest to life again.

Life a Property of Matter. Intelligence a Property of Matter, and infinite capacities unrecognised. No fear therefore in becoming matter (being matter now) as that is only becoming that which is itself life and intelligence. These properties of matter then make evident the other Ideas, the other Nature, the Beyond or Whole Idea—Matter not all, a part of the Whole Idea, or part of the Beyond.

. . .

Matter itself accounts for or contains all the phenomena put down to divinity.

. . .

SL. I see that *this* life is entirely different to what I understand.

I see that the other Nature or Beyond is entirely different.

I see that the after is entirely different—as before birth was entirely different.

I see that the whole scheme is quite outside.

SL. A tree—an outside idea at one in itself.

SL. I do not say I pray or give me this: but I feel the intense desire of sun life just the same & even more.

SL. The Beyond or Whole (Matter doing it for me better than I understand) or Scheme doing all this for me perhaps in a better & more beautiful way than I can see.

SL. Yet present evils are *real*—Put both facets that I see.

SL. I cannot even construct a human to please me, nor with all imagination, nothing better than sun life.

SL. Sun Life. By the glowing dandelion: by the cut hawkweed: by the grasses—still the same intense desire.

. . .

SL. Omit the word prayer—*now* say to live with that beauty & its thought within.

SL. The Universe does not come into accord with any ethics or science known therefore I conclude—there are other ideas besides those known to me.

SL. Nature holds all things to explain herself

Nature herself, herself all things explains.

SL. This Life—this *now*—is itself beyond—Since it is an idea outside my ideas. I myself express an idea I do not understand

SL. Bird on tree—expressing an idea I do not understand: they are Beyond.

SL. I do not want the physical explanation of the tree or me but the idea. By the Beyond then I mean the Idea of the *Whole*: that would fill the sky. The mind is too big for this little earth, that is why I cannot fit it—the mind requires more. I cannot force it down to this garden, and square/wall it in with a scheme. So that the sun life prayer or desire is right—After the most rigid criticism, and sternest effort to overthrow it. Nor can I square it down to all the mind of the universe—animated or inanimate—the mind *will* think outside it. Nor can I square the mind down to itself.

. . .

Torture Many have died once: I have had the misery of dying many times & the presence of it for years.

Children neglected playing with street roughs. Slobbering food for months like an imbecile old man. Handkerchief—drop not able to pick up. Writing a letter—effort.

Carefully arrange to do a dozen things at one rising or going upstairs.

Chair to chair—no rest.

Neither lie stand walk sit without distress.

Nor stoop lest kill me—like runners in the East, thrown down ring, pick up.

Beyond Quite outside & different to mind.

SL. Beyond. Hope in it while living.

. . .

SL. Tendency of modern thought to drag all things towards death & consider that only, or as chief.

. . .

SL. Religion Politics have no real meaning—counters with which the game of life is played.

SL. I cannot understand why rain & hill deserted me.

****

SL. night. Feb 19th.

I do not believe one word of it—neither the philosophers of old [primum mobile] the religions of the world, nor the science of today—not one word of what I have been taught or read. The truth is I believe entirely different [expressed by the Beyond].

SL. Innate proof in the intense Sun Life.

SL. The aspiration in Sun Life was right—wrong to crystallise in prayer for anything.

SL. It is the pure aspiration of the mind that is right.

SL. There is more than I have imagined rather than less.

. . .

SL. Still more psyche—not less—That is the side I chose, the mind-psyche.

SL. Re-existence—not immortality of the same.

SL. In myself as myself possess all safety.

SL. The savage feels it beside his tumulus

SL. The Norseman dying sitting in the sun with his arms.

SL. The Beyond—the Other Nature. Different—fills the sky

SL. In the Beyond have perfect confidence

SL. I can still hear the buzz of the flies in Hodson Hedge.

SL. I sit with book in hand—a fly buzzes past; nothing explains the fly: hence it is dear more.

SL. M.S. not too much crystallising—lose the meaning else in words.

SL. I begin all again, striking out everything, fresh from the flower the sun & the mind.

The Dawn

THERE CAME to my bedside this morning a visitant that has been present at the bedside of everyone who has lived for ten thousand years. In the darkness I was conscious of a faint light not visible if I looked deliberately to find it, but seen sideways, and where I was not gazing. It slipped from direct glance as a shadow may slip from a hand-grasp, but it was there floating in the atmosphere of the room. I could not say that it shone on the wall or lit the distant corner. Light is seen by reflection, but this light was visible of itself like a living thing, a visitant from the unknown. The dawn was in the chamber, and by degrees this intangible and slender existence would enlarge and deepen into day. Ever since I used to rise early to bathe, or shoot, or see the sunrise, the habit has remained of waking at the same hour, so that I see the dawn morning after morning, though I may sleep again immediately. Sometimes the change of the seasons makes it broad sunlight, sometimes it is still dark; then again the faint grey light is there, and I know that the distant hills are becoming defined along the sky. But though so familiar, that spectral light in the silence has never lost its meaning, the violets are sweet year by year though never so many summers pass away; indeed, its meaning grows wider and more difficult as the time goes on. For think, this spectre of the light—light's double-ganger—has stood by the couch of every human being for thousands and thousands of years. Sleeping or waking, happily dreaming, or wrenched with pain, whether they have noticed it or not, the finger of this light has pointed towards them. When they were building the pyramids, five thousand years ago, straight the arrow of light shot from the sun, lit their dusky forms, and glowed on the endless sand. Endless as that desert sand may be, innumerable in multitude its grains, there was and is a ray of light for each. A ray for every invisible atom that dances in the air—for the million million changing facets of the million ocean waves. Immense as these numbers may be, they are not incomprehensible. The priestess at Delphi in her moment of inspiration declared that she knew the number of the sands. Such number falls into insignificance before the mere thought of light, its speed, its quantity, its existence over space, and yet the idea of light is easy to the mind. The mind is the priestess of the Delphic temple of our bodies, and sees and understands things for which language is imperfect, and notation deficient.

There is a secret alphabet in it to every letter of which we unconsciously assign a value, just as the mathematician may represent a thousand by the letter A. In my own mind the idea of light is associated with the colour yellow, not the yellow of the painters, or of flowers, but a quick flash. This quick bright flash of palest yellow in the thousandth of an instant reminds me, or rather conveys in itself, the whole idea of light—the accumulated idea of study and thought. I suppose it to be a memory of looking at the sun—a quick glance at the sun leaves some such impression on the retina. With that physical impression all the calculations that I have read, and all the ideas that have occurred to me, are bound up. It is the sign—the letter—the expression of light. To the builders of the pyramids came the arrow from the sun, tinting their dusky forms, and glowing in the sand. To me it comes white and spectral in the silence, a finger pointed, a voice saying, 'Even now you know nothing.' Five thousand years since they were fully persuaded that they understood the universe, the course of the stars, and the secrets of life and death. What did they know of the beam of light that shone on the sonorous lap of their statue Memnon? The telescope, the microscope, and the prism have parted light and divided it, till it seems as if further discovery were impossible. This beam of light brings an account of the sun, clear as if written in actual letters, for example stating that certain minerals are as certainly there as they are here. But when in the silence I see the pale visitant at my bedside, and the mind rushes in one spring back to the builders of the pyramids who were equally sure with us, the thought will come to me that even now there may be messages in that beam undeciphered. With a turn of the heliograph, a mere turn of the wrist, a message is easily flashed twenty miles to the observer. You cannot tell what knowledge may not be pouring down in every ray; messages that are constant and perpetual, the same from age to age. These are physical messages. There is beyond this just a possibility that beings in distant earths possessed of greater knowledge than ourselves may be able to transmit their thoughts along, or by the ray, as we do along wires. In the days to come, when a deeper insight shall have been gained into the motions and properties of those unseen agents we call forces, such as magnetism, electricity, gravitation, perhaps a method will be devised to use them for communication. If so, communication with distant earths is quite within reasonable hypothesis. At this hour it is not more impossible than the transmission of a message to the antipodes in a few minutes would have been to those who lived a century since. The inhabitants of distant earths may have endeavoured to communicate with us in this way for ought we know time after time. Such a message is possibly contained sometimes in the pale beam which comes to my bedside. That beam always impresses me with a profound, an intense and distressful sense of ignorance, of being outside the intelligence of the universe, as if there were a vast civilization in view and yet not entered. Mere villagers and rustics creeping about a sullen earth, we know nothing of the grandeur and intellectual brilliance of that civilization. This beam fills me with unutterable dissatisfaction. Discontent, restless longing, anger at the denseness of the perception, the stupidity with which we go round and round in the old groove till accident shows us a fresh field. Consider, all that has been wrested from light has been gained by mere bits of glass. Mere bits of glass in curious shapes— poor feeble glass, quickly broken, made of flint, of the flint that mends the road. To this almost our highest conceptions are due. Could we employ the ocean as a lens we might tear truth from the sky. Could the greater intelligences that dwell on the planets and stars communicate with us, they might enable us to conquer the disease and misery which bear down the masses of the world. Perhaps they do not die. The pale visitor hints that the stars are not the outside and rim of the universe, any more than the edge of horizon is the circumference of our globe. Beyond the star-stratum, what? Mere boundless space. Mind says certainly not. What then? At present we cannot conceive a universe without a central solar orb for it to gather about and swing around. But that is only because hitherto our positive, physical knowledge has gone no farther. It can as yet only travel as far as this, as analogous beams of light. Light comes from the uttermost bounds of our star system—to that rim we can extend a positive thought. Beyond, and around it, whether it is solid, or fluid, or ether, or whether, as is most probable, there exist things absolutely different to any that have come under eyesight yet is not known. May there not be light we cannot see? Gravitation is an unseen light; so too magnetism; electricity or its effect is sometimes visible, sometimes not. Besides these there may be more delicate forces not instrumentally demonstrable. A force, or a wave, or a motion—an unseen light—may at this moment be flowing in upon us from that unknown space without and beyond the stellar system. It may contain messages from thence as this pale visitant does from the sun. It may outstrip light in speed as light outstrips an arrow. The more delicate, the more ethereal, then the fuller and more varied the knowledge it holds. There may be other things beside matter and motion, or force. All natural things known to us as yet may be referred to those two conditions: One, Force; Two, Matter. A third, a fourth, a fifth—no one can say how many conditions— may exist in the ultra-stellar space, beyond the most distant stars. Such a condition may even be about us now unsuspected. Something which is neither force nor matter is difficult to conceive; the mind cannot give it tangible shape even as a thought. Yet I think it more than doubtful if the entire universe, visible and invisible, is composed of these two. To me it seems almost demonstrable by rational induction that the entire universe must consist of more than two conditions. The grey dawn every morning warns me not to be certain that all is known. Analysis by the prism alone has quite doubled the knowledge that was previously available. In the light itself there may still exist as much more to be learnt, and then there may be other forces and other conditions to be first found out and next to tell their story. As at present known, the whole system is so easy and simple, one body revolving round another, and so on; it is as easy to understand as the motion of a stone that has been thrown. This simplicity makes me misdoubt. Is it all? Space—immeasurable space—offers such possibilities that the mind is forced to the conclusion that it is not, that there must be more. I cannot think that the universe can be so very very easy as this.

A Jefferies Bibliography

George Miller and Hugoe Matthews' *Richard Jefferies: A bibliographical study* (Scolar Press, 1993) provides the Jefferies scholar with an indispensable descriptive bibliography. The following list gives (1) the titles and dates of the first editions of Jefferies' chief books, published during his lifetime and posthumously, and (2) a selection of books about or containing significant discussions of Jefferies and his work.

1. Books by Richard Jefferies

The Scarlet Shawl, A Novel, 1874
Restless Human Hearts, A Novel, 1875
World's End: A Story in Three Books, 1877
The Gamekeeper At Home: Sketches of Natural History and Rural Life, 1878
Wild Life in a Southern County, 1879
The Amateur Poacher, 1879
Greene Ferne Farm, 1880
Hodge and His Masters, 1880
Round About a Great Estate, 1880
Wood Magic, A Fable, 1881
Bevis: The Story of a Boy, 1882
Nature Near London, 1883
The Story of My Heart: My Autobiography, 1883
Red Deer, 1883
The Life of the Fields, 1884
The Dewy Morn, A Novel, 1884
After London; Or, Wild England, 1885
The Open Air, 1885
Amaryllis at the Fair, A Novel, 1887
Field and Hedgerow, Being the Last Essays of Richard Jefferies, Collected by his Widow, 1889
The Toilers of the Field, 1892
The Hills and the Vale, with an introduction by Edward Thomas, 1909

The Nature Diaries and Note-Books of Richard Jefferies, edited with an
introduction and notes by Samuel J. Looker, 1948

The Old House At Coate and other hitherto unpublished essays by Richard
Jefferies, edited with an Introduction and Notes by Samuel J. Looker,
1948

Field and Farm, Essays Now First Collected, with Some from MSS. by
Richard Jefferies, edited with an Introduction and Notes by Samuel J.
Looker, 1957

Landscape & Labour, Essays and Letters Now First Collected with an
Introduction, Notes and Bibliography by John Pearson, 1979

2. Books about or containing discussions of the life and work of Richard Jefferies

The Eulogy of Richard Jefferies, Sir Walter Besant, Chatto and Windus, 1888

Richard Jefferies: A Study, H. S. Salt, Swan Sonnenschein and Co., 1894

Richard Jefferies: His Life and Work, Edward Thomas, Hutchinson and Co.,
1909

Richard Jefferies: Selections of his Work, with Details of his Life and
Circumstance, his Death and Immortality, Henry Williamson, Faber and
Faber, 1937

Richard Jefferies, Man of the Fields, Samuel J. Looker, Crichton Porteous,
John Baker, 1965

Richard Jefferies: A Critical Study, W. J. Keith, Oxford University
Press/University of Toronto Press, 1965

The Country and the City, Raymond Williams, Chatto and Windus, 1973

Lawrence and the Nature Tradition: A Theme in English Fiction 1859-1914,
Roger Ebbatson, Harvester Press, 1980

Tongues in Trees: Studies in Literature & Ecology, Kim Taplin, Green Books,
1989

The Entangled Eye: Visual Perception and the Representation of Nature in
Post-Darwinian Narrative, James Krasner, Oxford University Press, 1992

The Forward Life of Richard Jefferies, Hugoe Matthews, Phyllis Treitel,
Petton Books, 1994

Writers in a Landscape, Jeremy Hooker, University of Wales Press, 1996